I0152613

# DEDICATION

*To all who seek to walk
paths of strength and goodwill,
paths of clear sight and wisdom,
paths that honor our common life on this Earth.*

*This is the Earth we have.
This is the time we have.
These are the companions we have.*

*Let us make the most of our gifts,
our strength, our wisdom, our vision:
in the time we have, in the place we are,
with the people who are around us.*

*Let us walk a path that honors Heathen ways today,
and shines that honor out into a wider World.*

*Let us walk a path that honors Heathen ways today,*
*and shines that honor out into a wider World.*

# Oaths, Shild, Frith, Luck & Wyrd

## Five Essays Exploring
## Heathen Ethical Concepts
## and their Use Today

### Winifred Hodge Rose

TM

Wordfruma Press
2022

© 2022 Winifred Hodge Rose. All rights reserved. Brief quotations with full citation are permitted, for the purposes of criticism, teaching, or scholarship.

Wordfruma Press
PO Box 17343
Urbana Illinois 61803 USA

WordfrumaPress.com

ISBN
979-8-9855536-5-9 (Paperback)
979-8-9855536-6-6 (EPUB)

Library of Congress Control Number: 2022920109

This book may be ordered from:
https://www.lulu.com/shop

# Table of Contents

# 1. Introduction: A View of Heathen Ethics

Modern Heathen practice ranges along a spectrum running from strict retro-Heathen approaches to very modernized ones. Retro-Heathens seek to practice as closely as possible to what we know of old Heathen times, often choosing a particular Heathen culture such as Anglo-Saxons, Goths, or other tribal groups as their model. Modernized Heathens are more adapted to the perspectives of their 'host culture' and worldview. During more than thirty years of being Heathen, I have had experience with Heathen practices across this spectrum, and have gained and learned much thereby.

Among the important lessons I have learned is that there is a great deal of value in the old Heathen ways, including their ethical perspectives and folkways, and it is very much worthwhile to seek to understand them better. At the same time, history shows the inevitable problems and difficulties of some of their approaches, which is true of any society, anywhere and any time. No society is able to reach and maintain a perfectly balanced ethical system. Added to this is the fact that society and culture have changed a great deal since Heathen times, and we all need to live and function in this world today. Whatever ethical approaches we adopt need to take these considerations into account.

The word 'ethics' comes from the Greek *ethos*, which refers to 'customs, character, nature'. *Ethos* is used in English to mean "the characteristic spirit of a culture, era, or community as manifested in its beliefs and aspirations" (Oxford Languages). Put simply, ethics at root means 'the way things are customarily done; the right way to do things based on our own society's customs.' Let's explore this in a Heathen context now.

In my understanding, there are two interrelated areas of particular importance in Heathen ethics. One is the growth and maintenance of ethical personal power, or might and main: the inner strength and drive that is necessary to develop and sustain a good character and reputation, and to achieve worthy deeds during our life.

The second is the pursuit of relationships and community life that promote individual, group, and community well-being and effective functionality. Any thoughtful reading of Heathen history, old texts, tales, poems and sagas will show how important these two factors were in ancient Heathen life, and will show their complex interactions. This was generally illustrated by showing the painful, cascading disruptions that were caused by failures of, and transgressions against, these ethical values and aspirations.

I see 'might and main' as a common thread that ties together the subject matter of the five essays in this book. *Might*, as in *mighty, powerful*, is a familiar term in modern English. *Main*, as it is used here, is less so. It is the descendant of Anglo-Saxon *mægen*, Old Norse *megin*. It refers to power, but is also related to virtue and ethics. *Mægen* is defined as *strength, power, vigor, valor, virtue, efficacy, a good deed, a miraculous event (and the power behind it)*. Modern

Heathens often use this term in reference to spiritual and moral power. Thus, 'might and main' refer to all the powers of our being: physical, spiritual, mental, moral, the power of our will and of our vision.

I believe that elder Heathen ethics were based upon these powers of might and main, and how they can be developed and applied in daily life. Ethical persons use their might and main in ways that benefit themselves and their communities.

In this book, I explore specific concepts that were of central importance to elder Heathens, and discuss how they can be used in our own lives as modern Heathens seeking to grow and use our own ethical might and main for the betterment of ourselves and our world.

## Oaths

### A path to support Heathen might and main: growing personal power.

This was a practice that was much honored in the past and is something that I believe is often missing in today's culture. Ancient Heathens swore oaths: oaths of loyalty, oaths to accomplish certain deeds, oaths to support their reputations and their relationships. Such commitments shaped the circumstances of their lives.

Oaths can serve to strengthen one's will, one's character, one's relationships. Failed oaths and commitments, on the other hand, were and are very damaging to ourselves, to our relationships and reputation. Fulfilled oaths and commitments strengthen our spiritual power, our might and main, while failed oaths erode our strength of character and inner power.

My essays *Oaths: What They Mean and Why They Matter,* and *The Practice of Oathing,* offer a modern Heathen perspective on the nature and power of oaths and boasts, with cautions and advice about how to build one's personal power, one's mægen or main, to follow this Heathen path safely and to best effect.

## Shild

### *Wounded might and main; healing personal power.*

Anglo-Saxon *scyld* or *shild* meant, among other things, moral obligation, debt, responsibility for wrongdoing. All of us, at some time or another, make mistakes, fail at something that has bad consequences for us and others, commit wrongs. As well as doing these ourselves, others also do such things in ways that have harmful consequences for us. Things go wrong, luck turns against us, we feel like our life is unraveling. What should Heathens do, in such circumstances? How do we deal with guilt, with regret, with harm done by us, and to us? These are important questions within any religious and philosophical context.

In my essay *Threads of Wyrd and Scyld: A Ninefold Rite of Life Renewal,* I offer background and guidance for a Heathen ritual to address problems in life that are caused by wyrd and shild, either inherited or self-created, that are damaging one's life. I discuss the concept of wergild: methods to recompense and rebalance the harm that may have been caused by our actions and / or the actions of our forebears that still affect us today.

This Heathen rite is designed to address ethical questions such as: I have done something wrong, or my kin have done something wrong, or a wrong has been done to me that I have carried forward in my own life and affected others wrongly thereby; now what should I do about it? My luck, my ørlög, my wyrd, have gone askew: why is this happening? How shall I remedy this?

# Frith

### *Interwoven might and main: the roots of relationship and community.*

Ethics, customs, 'good' behavior at root support the social fabric, the web of relationships and interactions that make up a healthy and well-functioning community. The old word 'frith,' often translated as 'peace,' describes this web of relationships that maintains the peace and the many social goods that result from such a state. (My own name, Winifred or Wine-frith in its older form, means 'friend of frith, friend of peaceful interactions'.)

Oaths fulfilled support frith; forsworn or failed oaths damage it. When wrong behavior damages frith, then it's important to find ways to restore frith between ourselves and others whom we relate to. Frith, in many places and circumstances of our times, is something that is severely threatened or lacking altogether.

It is worthwhile taking a look at this old concept of frith, its roots in the past, and the way it shapes itself today, to get a clearer idea of its meaning and its value for human society. This is what I undertake in my essay *Heathen Frith and Modern Ideals.*

This essay begins by discussing the ancient roots of Heathen frith—the fabric which weaves together and maintains a community, however small or large. It goes on to discuss the role of frith in religious conversion, the newer roots of frith in modern ideals, and describes some of the pitfalls that can arise in the pursuit of frith. The overall focus is to become aware of the dynamics of frith, both positive and negative, so as to pursue it mindfully and to best effect.

## Luck and Wyrd

*Flows of might and main: hidden paths of Heathen wisdom.*

'Luck' is a mysterious phenomenon; it is something that was of great importance to Heathens in the past. Why? What is luck, what influences it, how does it increase or decrease? What is the connection between luck and ethics, if any? What about the connection between ethics, luck and fate or wyrd?

My essay *Webs of Luck and Wyrd: Interplays and Impacts on Events* provides an overview of the complex beliefs about luck in some of the ancient Heathen cultures. It examines traditional views of luck and wyrd through the lens of Heathen history, seeking insights into the influences of these concepts in wars, conflicts, and the political processes of the conversion from Heathenism to Christianity. This essay draws lessons that we can apply today, concerning the roles of luck, wyrd and wisdom in our life.

# Applied Heathen ethics

Any system of ethics, from any time and place in the world, is nuanced, complex, subject to fluctuations and change. This is because human nature and the circumstances of human life are nuanced, complex, and subject to change! Ethical ideals need to provide us with structure and stability as a basis for conducting our personal and social lives. At the same time, they need to fit us, fit our nature, they need to be something we can work with, that enhances our well-being. Ethics are ideals that we strive toward, but must also be patterns that we can live with, without distortion of our inner or outer self.

To achieve such a delicate ethical balance between inner personal needs, and outer community needs, requires *wisdom*, another quality that was greatly admired by ancient Heathens, and often seems to have fallen by the wayside today. The full expression of Heathen wisdom requires not only knowledge, experience, and insight. It also requires a deep understanding of Heathen metaphysics, of the hidden workings of wyrd, ørlög, the cosmic powers, of spiritual beings such as the Deities and ancestors, and the inner powers of Earth, Nature, and the Otherworlds.

Wisdom requires the long view through time and space, this-worldly and otherworldly phenomena, personal and other-centered space. It requires the commitment of all our faculties: thought, reason, analysis, synthesis, imagination, intuition, sensory and emotional processing, patience, hindsight, foresight, memory, and dream.

Another quality that is implied throughout the discussion of Heathen ethics here is *generosity:* a generosity of spirit which acknowledges that the ethics of living with and working with a community are worthwhile. It is worthwhile to build our own reputation and self-respect within a larger whole of also respecting others, their needs and deeds. It is worthwhile to mend our relationships and interactions when they go wrong. It is worthwhile to weave frith, and keep re-weaving it as necessary. It is worthwhile to teach these ways to our youth, to guide them toward Heathen values and wisdom, while allowing them the freedom to explore their own paths through this landscape. Generosity means making space within the web of frith for others as well as for ourselves and those closest to us.

Let's move on now, to a closer examination of something that is very meaningful to the Heathen way of life: how to grow, maintain, heal, and share the personal power, the soul-might and spiritual strength, that we can achieve by walking a Heathen path with trust, wisdom and determination. All of the essays in this book, whatever their actual subject matter, also address this underlying message of Heathen ethics: *following an ethical path leads to strength of character and strength of soul.*

8

*Fulfilled oaths build Heathen might and main,
increasing our personal power.*

*Unpaid shild wounds our might and main;
taking responsibility for shild heals personal power.*

*Frith is a fabric of interwoven might and main,
created and shared by many:
the roots of relationship and community.*

*Luck and wyrd can be expressed through flows of
might and main, discovered along the complex,
hidden paths that lead to Heathen wisdom.*

*Step forth now to meet the challenge!*

Thor's Hammer with attached Oath Ring, made by my husband, blacksmith Rosten Dean Rose. The ring is made from an antique lightning rod, twisted with copper. We swore our wedding oaths on this Hammer and Oath Ring, and our marriage is still strong after more than 20 years.

# 2. Oaths

## What They Mean and Why They Matter

*Heathen might and main: Growing personal power.*

What is an oath? In the belief of many modern Heathens, a true oath is a statement whose implications and essence have actually been laid in the Well of Wyrd, becoming an integral part of orlay or ørlög. The true oath becomes part of the pattern of That-Which-Is, thus gaining the power to shape That-Which-Is-Becoming, and That-Which-Should-Be, the respective domains of the three Norns: Urdh, Verðandi, Skuld. By laying the oath in the Well, the deed or deeds done in fulfilment of one's oath should also 'fall into' the Well and become a part of orlay. In this way, one seeks to establish a deeper meaning and significance to one's life, to ensure that one's deeds—even if they are later forgotten—nevertheless form a permanent part of the fabric of reality.

Ancient Heathens placed the highest possible value on the survival of their reputations beyond their own deaths, which spurred them to perform mighty deeds heedless of fear or the cost to themselves. They trusted to their poets, scops and skalds to ensure that their reputation survived through the ages. In our day, modern Heathens may well feel somewhat doubtful about how many generations the telling of many of our own deeds will survive, which may discourage

11

some from valuing mighty deeds and great reputations as much as our forebears did.

Now, a word about such 'great deeds': think carefully about what this means for us today. Facing enemies in battle may be something some of us are called on to do, but behind that, below, above, and around that, is the important need to face the challenges of everyday life, to work to make life better for ourselves and others, whatever it takes.

There are so many other needs within our families, our communities, our workplaces, our neighborhoods, the natural environment around us, and the world as a whole. The world cries out for deeds of great-heartedness, generosity, wisdom, foresight; deeds that contribute to wellbeing for all, deeds that heal, protect, support, renew the world around us, and renew the courage, strength and hope of those whose lives we touch. These are deeds that Heathen oaths can empower us to achieve, and that live on in all the lives we have touched.

A deep understanding of the nature of oaths, and the connections between oaths, deeds, and orlay, provides great reassurance for today's Heathens that we can indeed make our deeds—all worthy deeds, no matter how unexciting they may seem—and our lives count for something worthwhile, regardless of whether they are consciously remembered for countless ages or not.

How does one 'lay' one's oaths and deeds in the Well? There is no way to guarantee that this will happen; orlay is not under our ultimate control. But the swearing of oaths in sumbel, over holy drink or on an oath ring, and sealed by asking the witness of our own Holy Ones and folk, makes it likely that the oath will indeed be laid in the Well. As time progresses it is often possible to see, both by obvious evidence as well as more hidden signs discerned through runecasting, thyle's work, and spaecraft, whether the oath is a true one, laid in the Well, or not.

Then when one's deed is accomplished, or one wishes to boast the living of one's life in accordance with one's oaths, boasts describing one's deeds should again be given in sumbel to enhance the likelihood of the deeds falling into the Well, in truth. As I believe, this process involves not only the Well of Wyrd, but Mimir's Well also—the repository of collective memory. This is one reason for the taking of oaths and boasting of them in public, in the assembly of the folk at holy sumbel: so that the memory of what one swears and what one does can be laid in collective memory, the gateway to Mimir's Well.

## Kinds of Oaths and Boasts

There are several different categories of oaths, all of them powerful and meaningful. One category is the *boast,* a statement made and sworn to, usually in sumbel, that generally applies to the achievement of a specific deed. The boast also refers to *reporting the accomplishment of that deed,* so that there is a 'boast to do' something and a 'boast that you have done' that thing. Both steps of the process are important: they are the initiation and the closure of the deed, and neither the deed nor the boast are complete unless both are steps are 'reported.' Again, it is important that these are done at sumbel, rather than in a less formal and holy setting, if at all possible.

Another type of oath involves swearing to adhere to *certain standards of behavior.* This kind of oath may be required for certain offices or positions of responsibility, including leaders of organizations, kindreds, hearths, guilds and other groups. Rather than involving a specific deed that has a beginning and an end, the oath of behavior continues indefinitely, for as long as one holds the position that requires that kind of behavior. This kind of oath is also administered during sumbel, whenever possible.

It is very appropriate for a person's friends or those who have benefited from that person's performance of office to stand up in sumbel and boast this person's deeds from time to time. One can certainly also do this for oneself as well, for example by saying: "I swore this oath a year ago, and have kept to the terms faithfully, even in the face of difficulties"— and proceed to boast the overcoming of those difficulties.

In our 'host culture,' boasting one's own behavior in such a way generally is considered inappropriate. But according to our own folkways it is an essential part of building one's Heathen soul, strengthening the ties between Heathens as a community, and increasing the power of Heathen main (soul-power) and workings in the world by laying more Heathen orlay in the Well. One of the important functions of boasting is also to set an example for others. All of us benefit from the inspiring examples of others, and Heathen gatherings are a good place to bring such examples to the fore.

A third kind I call an *oath of relationship,* and in this category there are two kinds of relationship. One is the relationship of an individual to a group, the obvious example being a kindred member's loyalty to the whole group. Some Heathen groups have such an oath required as a condition of membership, though many do not. Such an oath is often taken in a special ceremony for that specific purpose, and may involve sumbel as well as perhaps other rituals.

The second oath of relationship is an oath between two individuals, and again here there are several different sub-categories: oaths of kinship such as blood-siblinghood, adoption, and fostering; marriage oaths; hold-oaths of fealty; and a large category of less rigidly-defined oaths that one might lump together as friendship oaths.

As in the case of oaths of behavior, it is very important to make opportunities to boast one's oaths of relationship in sumbel from time to time, for the same reasons. The anniversaries of the oath are especially suitable times for boasting it. In ancient times, people made a great point of rewarding hold-oaths in this way, by boasting the deeds and the loyalty of sworn warriors toward their lord or lady, and rewarding them with gifts. This was indeed one of the primary ways of payment for the warrior's services, and praise counted as much as gold did!

It is very appropriate for those who have sworn an oath of relationship, such as a married couple, to boast one another at sumbel, and perhaps exchange gifts at the same time. This action strengthens and celebrates the relationship, as well as helping to lay the deeds (perhaps simply the quiet, everyday deeds of love, help, and loyalty) into the Well as they deserve to be laid.

## Oaths, Wyrd and Luck

Making and fulfilling oaths and boasts is a powerful and quintessentially Heathen way to align oneself actively with the flow of wyrd. Though there is no power in any world that can wrest control of wyrd out of the hands of the Norns, nevertheless one can have a significant effect on the shape and direction of one's wyrd through the action of oathing and living the oath.

To use an analogy, think of a sailor. The power of the sea is greater than any individual person is, and no human can hope to overcome or direct this power by brute force alone. But by the application of wisdom, insight, skill, courage and steadfastness, one can sense the flows and patterns, the natural movements of the sea's forces, and use that knowledge to align oneself with them. By that alignment, one is able to ride the wave through all obstacles to reach one's desired goal.

This ability to align oneself with wyrd and with natural forces is closely akin to luck. One's success in doing so, or lack thereof, will result in an oath that all can recognize as being 'lucky' or 'unlucky.' The willingness to discern and align oneself with the patterns of wyrd through one's oaths is a living expression of Heathen belief in the action of wyrd—an affirmation of our faith in the strongest way possible, by the way we choose to live our lives.

# Oaths and the Heathen Soul

On the personal level, the ability to take and keep oaths of all kinds is an expression of one's personal soul-power, one's main. Oaths arise from the vitality of the Heathen soul, from a sense of overflowing vigor, confidence, eagerness. As the athlete or warrior delights in strength and skill, as the crafter exults in the abundance of the gift to create, so the Heathen heart and soul, rich in main, yearns to challenge and channel that main along the stringent, shining pathway that is laid out by the taking of an oath.

Certain soul-qualities are necessary for oath-taking. Wisdom is the most essential. Oaths are absolutely nothing to play with or play at; the consequences of foolish oath-taking are too severe both for oneself and for one's community. One must have an understanding of the interactions between oaths, wyrd, and one's own orlay, an understanding of the effects of the oath on one's community, and of the personal implications of an oath, before committing to it. Wisdom requires a deep level of self-knowledge, and good knowledge of the other person or persons involved in the oath, if it is an oath of relationship.

Consider what impact the new oath might have on any existing oaths you are bound to. Will the new oath interfere with the accomplishment of older oaths? Will it create new relationships that could conflict with existing relationships, oathed or not? Are you clearly free to take the new oath, or do bonds of an existing oath prevent you from doing so? Think ahead before oathing, and find solutions for any such problems before committing yourself to the oath.

Though the final decision is yours alone, do not hesitate to seek the counsel of wise Heathens whom you trust, as you prepare to take your oath.

Steadfastness and self-confidence are also necessary. Steadfastness and self-confidence may need to be built up slowly in one's character, much as an athlete builds muscle and flexibility. If you have a history of failing at or abandoning your life's tasks and responsibilities, if your self-confidence is low, or if you are a very young person still developing your character, it is wise to begin challenging yourself with small, short-term, easy-to-accomplish (but nevertheless meaningful) oaths and boasts.

Each successful accomplishment will build your main, your personal power, and lay more of your deeds in the orlay of the Well, enabling you to increase the challenge you set yourself in the next oath or boast you make. Build up your main, your soul-strength, your steadfastness and self-confidence, in this way until your heart and soul are full to abundance with these qualities, eager for the challenge of truly mighty oaths.

## Oaths and the Community

A community is a fabric woven of many threads of relationship and commonality, forming a recognizable whole with a distinctive pattern. The whole fabric may be strong or weak, its patterns may be strikingly beautiful, or dull and nondescript, or jaggedly clashing, depending on the qualities of the threads and how they are woven. If the fabric is well-woven and strong, this fabric can be seen as frith itself: a distinctively patterned kind of relationship evolved by our Heathen forebears which is still of great value to us today.

Oaths play a very important role in the weaving and maintenance of the fabric of community and of frith. By the same token, destructive oaths, foolish or unlucky oaths, or the failure of constructive oaths can cause severe or fatal damage to the fabric of relationships and hence of community. This is most especially true of Heathen communities, because of the central importance to us of the interweavings of oaths, wyrd, and the orlays of individuals, families, kindreds and communities. Any Heathen who is familiar with the famous Norse and Germanic sagas and tales can come up with many examples of this truth.

As only one example, think of the fatal tangles woven around the oaths taken by Siglinde, Sigmund, Brunnhilde (Sigdrifa) the Valkyrie, Sigfried, Gudrun, Gundahari, Hagan and others in the *Volsunga Saga* and the *Nibelungenlied*. The tangled oaths led to the loss and destruction of individuals, families, and entire tribes and folkdoms, as well as the loss and destruction of love and loyalties among them. Oaths, their wisdom or unwisdom, luck or unluck, played a pivotal role in these dramatic developments. Today's Heathens who seek wisdom in oath-taking will do well to study carefully the role played by oaths in the sagas and other tales of all the Germanic peoples.

It may be that such study will daunt many of us, and make us hesitant to take oaths for fear of dreadful consequences. To my way of thinking, however, the alternative is no more attractive or inspiring. A Heathen who is fearful or hesitant to make a boast or take an oath, after careful thought and preparation, is living only a shadow of true Heathen life. The soul-power and main that is developed by the taking and fulfilling of mighty oaths will die still-born, or grow to be spindly and weak, in such an individual. Under such circumstances a person's self-development along the distinctive pathways of our faith is handicapped.

Great deeds can indeed be done without recourse to boasts and oaths. However, boasting and oathing are mechanisms to help ensure that the greatest amount of main is gained from the deed, and that these deeds are laid in the Wells and woven into the wyrd of the world. Main is generated both for the individual and for the folk by following the complete 'life cycle' of oathing: (1) boast/oath 'to do', (2) deed done, and (3) boast of 'have done.' So, when circumstances allow, it is ideal to proceed with this complete cycle. In the case of spur-of-the-moment deeds, where no oath was made to do the deed beforehand, the deed should still be boasted in sumbel afterwards, so that it is planted in the memories and inspiration of one's community.

In the same way that the wyrd of an individual can be affected either by the making of, or the failure to make oaths and boasts, so also the wyrd of one's community is affected. The bonds of community are in large part made up of oaths, or of oath-like commitments, including marriage oaths, commitments to one's children, parents and other kin that are as strong as oaths even if they are not spoken, partnerships for community-enhancing purposes, commitments of loyalty and troth to other folk and to Holy Ones, and many other such commitments. Making oaths, boasts and commitments foolishly or unluckily, or failing to keep one's oaths, can badly tangle the wyrd of one's community, as we can see in the sagas and in history.

But on the other side, failing to make oaths, boasts of great deeds, and other worthy commitments, leaves us with nothing at all, no roots or foundations, no strong walls to build on, just an empty void. We can see obvious examples of all of these problems in the everyday society of our own times, in noting what happens to the community, small or large, when marriage oaths are broken, commitments to children, parents and kin neglected, friendships and partnerships betrayed, the commitments of good citizenship ignored, when people break their word or have no 'word' left to break, when boasts are empty air, and there is nothing in which to trust, nothing which inspires one to greatness.

## Between the Fire and the Ice

It is easy to think, with respect to oaths and boasts, that we are caught between a rock and a hard place: should we choose commitments with all their risks, or the emptiness of the uncommitted life? Let me point out, however, that this is the kind of environment in which the true Heathen thrives and comes into full power! This is our 'niche' in the ecology of the world, the place we are adapted to fill and to excel in. There is a sword's edge, a thread's span, between the fire and the ice: between the destruction and chaos caused by wrong oath-taking or failed oaths on one side, and the gray nothingness of a life without oaths and boasts on the other.

21

That sword's edge, that thread's span, is our own path: the Heathen way.

To walk this path we must apply our powers of deep wisdom, courage, high-heartedness, vision, and faith. We must have strong main, soul-power, as individuals and as part of a thriving community, a wholeness. We cannot walk this path alone: what meaning has an oath, if the one making it is the only one in the world? An oath, and the deeds that follow from it, have no context, have little meaning or significance, if they are not ultimately made to and for one's community. By wisely making and holding to our oaths and boasts, one of the great things we accomplish is the stronger weaving of our bonds of community and our trust in one another: Gods and folk, together.

*The words of Sigrdrifa the Valkyrie,*
*spoken to Sigurd after he awakened her:*

*"Hear my rede: Do not swear an oath unless it is truly kept."*

(The Lay of Sigrdrifa, v. 23, in the Poetic Edda; my rendition.)

# 3. The Practice of Oathing

Oathing can gain us might and main, support our relationships, strengthen us in the face of challenges and hardships, build our character and reputation, and provide a channel for the flow of luck in our life. Mistaken or failed oaths can create chaos and unluck in our life and the lives of others who are involved with us. (See *Webs of Luck and Wyrd* in this book for more about the flow of luck.)

Here, I want to discuss how to help yourself succeed in oathing, and how to be aware of what can go wrong with oathing so you can practice this skill wisely. Here are some basic principles for you to consider, which I will elaborate on in the following sections.

1. Be realistic; start with small and easy oaths, and gradually build up to more challenging ones after you have succeeded with easier oaths.

2. As much as possible, design and word your oath so that your achievement of it depends on you, not on anyone else, or on making assumptions about what might or might not happen in the future. In other words, you want the achievement of your oath to be under your own control.

3. If you're considering an oath of relationship, an oath to another person, group, or organization, do your homework

first and give it plenty of time before you decide. Get to know the person well, over a longer period of time. Find out more about the group, its leaders, its history, its interactions with others. Trust your instincts, if something seems 'off' to you. Err on the side of caution, until you have known them long enough to be able to judge wisely.

4. The wording of your oath is of great importance, and can make or break your likelihood of success. This is truly an art-form, and requires thought, wisdom, and self-knowledge. I advise never to make a spur-of-the-moment, unconsidered oath, except under the most extreme circumstances of necessity and responsibility. Under normal circumstances, always take the time to consider and word the oath well.

Let's discuss these suggestions in more depth now.

## First Steps in Oathing Practice

1. **Begin your practice with something relatively easy**, that can be accomplished within a specified timeframe, but choose something that has value to you. For example: "I will read this book that looks so interesting within the next month." Or: "I will make sure I have a gift for my loved one in time for their birthday; I won't forget or be late."

2. Once you've decided on your oath, **speak it or write it formally** in your journal or on a note card that you post or keep handy. Consider that you are saying this not only to

yourself, but to your Gods and Goddesses, your ancestors if you wish, and / or any other well-intentioned beings such as landwights, if relevant. Make a little ceremony of this speaking or writing. *The oath should be formally expressed,* though you can keep it totally private if you wish.

3. Along with your oath, you should **decide on the shild you will pay if you fail in your oath.** This shild is a penalty, a fail-safe, a way to partially remedy the effects of a failed oath on your might and main and your ørlög. It won't entirely remedy a failure, though; this is not a 'get out of jail free' card! You really, really don't want to have to resort to this! But sometimes circumstances beyond your control may cause you to fail or partially fail in your oath.

The shild you choose should match or exceed the 'power level' of your oath. If the oath is relatively easy and simple, the shild can be relatively low-key in terms of time, effort, value, but it should still be a meaningful price or penalty.

If the oath is powerful and serious, the shild should be something that is really costly to you in some way. For example: giving up something that means a lot to you, making a substantial donation to a charity in an amount where you feel the financial pinch, or performing an act of service that is a real sacrifice of time and effort. Speak or write the shild you decide upon, along with the oath. (The next chapter in this book, *Threads of Wyrd and Shild,* has more information about shild.)

4. *And then do it!* **Accomplish the oath in the timeframe that you set yourself.** Failing to accomplish the oath is worse for your might and main than not oathing at all. Failing to set a timeframe, or exceeding the timeframe before you accomplish your oath, means that you get away with putting off the oath indefinitely, which defeats the purpose!

5. **When you have accomplished your oath, celebrate it.** If you can boast it in sumble, great! Or you can do this alone: stand in front of your altar or other suitable place, and raise a 'horn' (or a cup or mug of whatever drink you choose) and speak your boast to yourself and to your Gods, Goddesses, and include ancestors if you choose. If your surroundings make it difficult to do this openly, then do it in your imagination and your heart.

6. Once you've achieved that oath, **set yourself another one,** perhaps a little more difficult than the first, and follow the same procedures. Keep doing this, using faithfully fulfilled oaths to build up your might and main, your personal power and self-confidence, and your strong, ethical character in accordance with Heathen practice. You are building powerful oath-muscles here!

## More Challenging Oaths

When you feel you have a good handle on the simpler oathing practice, you can move on to more difficult ones. For example:

*Breaking bad habits or addictions*

These are very difficult, challenging oaths to accomplish, and there are procedures developed by movements such as Alcoholics Anonymous that can help. It seems simple to break this down into small pieces: "I will not indulge in this habit or addiction for today," or even half a day. But even that can be very challenging for a strong addiction, or for a habit that is reinforced by people around you, your circumstances, the demands on you. For example, losing your temper when things go wrong, or breaking your diet because you have to cook for your whole family and it's too much trouble to make a separate meal. If you plan on using oathing to help you with these things, I strongly recommend these measures:

(a) First spend plenty of time on the kind of oathing I described before, which is easier to accomplish and will build your oathing-muscles and your self-confidence.

(b) Break the time-frame you use for your oath into tiny chunks. The more difficult the habit or addiction, the smaller the time-chunks. An hour, even half an hour. Though you probably can't do a formal oathing and boasting ceremony multiple times throughout your day, nevertheless pause briefly to make the oath in your heart, and then do not forget to acknowledge your achievement when the time is up.

(c) Set yourself up for success by not asking too much of yourself at once; be realistic, take baby steps here. But then

27

be sure to do it! For the health of your souls, your reputation, your character, your self-respect, *you must achieve your oath.* Make your oath achievable, and don't let yourself fail.

### Long-term and open-ended oaths

These are often commitments and oaths of relationship, such as marriage oaths, or the commitments between parents and children which may not be spoken but are as strong as the most powerful oaths. Many of these oaths are assumed and treated as lifetime oaths, especially kinship commitments, and usually marriage as well.

Others may be open-ended with regard to their time-frame, such as friendship oaths, where friends may swear an oath as to how they will treat each other, but not specify a time-frame. Friendships may last a lifetime, or may drift apart for various reasons, so it often makes sense to leave them open-ended, not specifying a time-frame for the oath.

Some people prefer to approach marriage oaths the same way: swear to treat each other in good ways and support the marriage and family, but leave the time-frame open-ended. Others prefer the stronger commitment of oathing for a lifetime, believing that such an oath is more supportive of their values and desires for their life and relationships.

## Oaths of Relationship

### Marriage / domestic partnership oaths

Building your oathing-muscles as I described earlier will help you improve the performance of such long-term commitments. Some people like to reaffirm their wedding-oaths at an appropriate time, such as their anniversary, and this is an excellent practice. You can reaffirm your original promises, or you can create together a new oath that reflects where you both are in your lives and your relationship today. This is especially good if your marriage or partnership has been under stress and needs to make a fresh start. The next chapter in this book, *Threads of Wyrd and Shild: A Ninefold Rite of Life-Renewal*, might offer some additional assistance for such circumstances.

### Unspoken kinship commitments

Except for marriage oaths, most kinship commitments go unexpressed, though they may be very powerful. I believe it is a good practice to formalize kinship commitments by oathing, even if this is just unspoken in your heart. When I witnessed the births of two of my grandsons, and the adoption of my third, very profound oaths of love and commitment arose in my heart, flowed forth as tears, and were formalized by a kiss upon their brow as I held them in my arms for the first time. These heart-oaths will never be broken.

When I realized that my mother was coming down with Alzheimer's, I made a formal oath to myself that I would walk that road with her to the end, offering all the care and companionship that I could. That oath helped to stabilize and strengthen me during the very difficult eleven years that followed.

## *Adoption and fostering*

The adoption or fostering of a child is a very suitable occasion for an oath of promise to love, guide, and care for the child, and prepare them for a good adult life. A formal adoption ceremony for such an event is a beautiful thing, where your oath to the child can be formally witnessed and supported by your kin and friends. Heathens in elder times sometimes adopted a child or an adult into the kindred, accompanied by a formal, public celebration to witness the event. Fostering was also widely practiced during elder times, and the responsibility of a person toward their fosterling was taken very seriously.

In today's world, step-parents might greatly benefit their new families by taking on such oaths and responsibilities toward their new step-children and other kin, whether done formally and openly, or done quietly in their hearts if family members would not be comfortable with such a ceremony.

## *Friendship and blood-siblinghood*

These oaths of the closest friendship ties can be of great value in one's life; as with all oaths, they should be approached seriously. Friendship oaths can be tailored to suit the relationship, for example a gentle oath stating how you will treat your friend, never lie to them, always listen to what they have to say, and the like.

Blood-siblinghood oaths are rare and demanding. They are intended to create true kinship between two people, who become as siblings to each other, and as family members

30

to each other's families and kindreds. Just as with kinship, siblinghood oaths are generally assumed to last for a lifetime, and should be approached with the utmost seriousness, after much time and thought about all the implications involved.

## Working partnerships

This kind of oath is seldom practiced today, yet I think it is one of great value, and recommend it for Heathen practice. Any time you decide to undertake a project or an enterprise with others, and especially with other Heathens, you could choose to express in an oath to each other how you will approach the work and treat each other. This is something like a contract, but a contract of 'giving your word' to each other instead of putting something into a formal written contract.

Note that the Anglo-Saxon word 'wed,' the same as our word 'wed, wedding,' did not only refer to a marriage agreement. The old 'wed' meant any kind of contract, bargain, or agreement, when people gave their word and intended it to be reliable. The fact that we use the word 'wed' today only for the most serious of modern oaths, the marriage oath, shows the power of this word 'wed'.

We should take the implications to heart: giving our word is a serious commitment. Our reputation rises or falls on our ability to accomplish what we say we will do. This is all part of building our might and main by Heathen oathing, and while doing so, weaving frith by coming together for a common purpose. (See my essay *Heathen Frith* in this book, for more about weaving frith.)

31

When we oath or seriously 'give our word' on projects with other Heathens, it is a great opportunity for each one to practice their oathing skills, gain might and main from oathing, and weave Heathen frith together, as well as setting up the project with a high likelihood of success! This also allows us to grow the 'power of our word,' of our reputation as a straight-speaker whose word and promise can be relied upon, something which was held in high honor in the past, and should be revived today.

This kind of project partnership can apply very widely: to volunteer work, business partnerships, projects on behalf of your Heathen group or organization, Heathen group activities, etc. It can be something short-term, long-term, or open-ended, depending on the type of project or enterprise you are engaged in.

## Oaths of Office or Duty

Some positions, especially those which serve the public in some way, require or expect either a formal oath, or an unwritten understanding about how we should conduct ourselves while working in that position. Doctors must swear the Hippocratic Oath. Military personnel swear oaths of service; police, fire-fighters and similar professions may also expect this. Members of Congress, state legislators, and judges swear oaths of office. Some Heathen groups and organizations require their officers to swear an oath. There are many other examples. We may, ourselves, choose to make an inner commitment to the spirit of service of our office, job, or duty, even if oaths are not required.

These oaths should be taken with the same degree of seriousness as any personal oaths we might consider, even though the requirement and the wording of the oath may not be up to us. If we are accepting that position, we must be willing to take any oath that is associated with it, and fulfill its requirements. Failing to fulfill our oath of office has the same unfortunate consequences on our wyrd as failing at any other type of oath, and may have mundane legal consequences as well.

## Oaths of Self-Commitment

Another type of oath is one that we make to ourself, perhaps quietly to ourself, or perhaps with the witness of others such as making an oath in sumbel. A common purpose for such an oath is to support us in achieving some important life goal, perhaps involving our career, or something we really want to do.

Often it isn't possible to predict or control when such opportunities may arise, so this type of oath may need to be open-ended, and worded appropriately. For example: "I will prepare myself for {doing this, whatever your goal is} by {this kind of training and preparation}, will be watchful for opportunities to fulfill this goal, and will follow up such opportunities with all my will in a timely manner." One of the things that might be necessary in these cases is saving money that would be needed to follow the opportunity, and that would be part of your oath.

This will help to direct your might and main, your intention, awareness, and luck, to maximize the likelihood of you attaining your goal. At the same time, it doesn't put you in an impossible bind by setting a time-limit on a situation and circumstances that may be beyond your control. You may not be able to force the opportunity you want to happen, nor control the timing of it if it does happen. What you are promising is that you will be watchful for such an opportunity and prepare yourself to follow up on it, when and if it does arise. And then you need to do what you promised!

## Wording your Oaths

The preceding example is a good segue into this section about how to word your oaths. It's very important to give serious thought to this; wording can make or break your success in oathing. Here are some guidelines for wording your oaths.

1. Think about the oath you want to make, and pay careful attention to what factors are under your control, and what factors are not. For example, in a relationship oath of any kind, you cannot control what the other person will do. You can only control what you will do. So word your oath accordingly, with 'I-statements.' **Always build the intention and the wording of your oath around factors that you control yourself.** Don't depend on, or make assumptions about, what other people will do, or what the future will bring. You are working with your own might and main and your own wyrd here; you need to be clear-sighted and realistic.

2. If at all possible, **focus on positive rather than negative wording.** For example, if you are using oathing to help you break a habit or addiction, don't say "I will not do {whatever it is} for the next hour, or the next day." This kind of wording will focus your mind, consciously and subconsciously, on depriving yourself and making yourself suffer, and this is hard to support over the long term.

Word your oath so that, instead of focusing on depriving yourself of something, you focus on **giving yourself a gift.** One that I like to use is the gift of freedom. So I might say "For the next hour, I will be free of the necessity to do {whatever it is}." Notice I do not say "free of the urge," because this may not be under our control, especially in the case of an addiction. Instead, I'm saying that I am free of the driving need, the necessity, to *act* on this urge. I don't *have* to do this, whatever it is. *I can choose to be free,* to act freely according to my will, not my need. I give myself the gift of freedom, and so, little by little, I replace the driving need that makes me unfree.

Taking an approach like this, we can see that while an oath might seem to be constricting and binding, in truth it can be constructed so that it actually frees us from bindings that are strangling us, right now.

Other gifts you might give yourself include the gifts of love, health, strength, cleanness, self-respect, praise and encouragement, and many more. I advise not to use material gifts, which have the possibility of just turning into another bad habit. Instead, gift yourself by deploying meaningful but non-material inner powers that will build your might and main, your health and strength, on all levels of your being.

These are the true gifts, given by yourself to yourself, as Odin did when he hung upon the Tree. These are esoteric mysteries that lead us toward an ethical, self-directed, power-filled Heathen life, supported by wise oathing.

3. Another guideline for wording your oaths wisely: **be realistic about what you really can do, and be specific about describing that in your oath.** Not all oaths need to be mighty, world-changing productions! You can use realistic, sensible oaths to re-tune your life, your actions and behavior, your goals, your relationships, in small ways as well as large.

You can just focus on changing one small thing, which may well turn out to have wider effects than you expected. This often happens, and it happens not just because of the small thing you changed, but because of the power, luck, might and main that fulfilling an oath gives to you and your life. Give this a try; you may be pleasantly surprised by how far the good effects can spread!

4. Consider whether it is realistic and helpful to **specify a time-frame** in the oath, or whether it will work better as an open-ended oath.

(a) It is helpful to put a *time-frame* on the oath when it is a specific deed or action to accomplish, and you want to ensure that you don't procrastinate about it. Also, the deed itself might have a natural time-frame, a time when the deed or action needs to be finished or accomplished. For example, producing some work you promised to do by a certain deadline.

Another reason to put a time-frame on the oath is when it is something difficult or strenuous, that you can't realistically keep up forever. An example here is the step-by-step measures you might take to overcome a bad habit. Another is your preparation for a grueling event or challenge, such as an athletic competition or studying for an important exam. After the event is over, your oath is also finished and can be boasted as done.

(b) Some types of oaths may work best if they are *open-ended*, with no time-frame. Many types of relationship oaths are like this: your oath will shape the conduct of that relationship for as long as it continues. But if that relationship comes to an end or drifts away, you and the other person or group are no longer bound by the oath, because you did not swear to keep it for a lifetime or a specific period of time. You only swore to conduct the relationship in a particular way, implying that the oath lasts for as long as the relationship lasts.

Another example is an oath of office: your promise to behave in a certain way while in that position may no longer be relevant, once you leave the position.

## Oathing Precautions

1. Give yourself plenty of time and thought before deciding on an oath, and ensure that your oaths are consistent with your own ethical values.

2. Base all your oathing on your own decisions and timing. Do not allow anyone else to pressure you into an oath before you are ready, or if you are unsure about it.

3. Pay close attention to the wording of your oath, and if this is a shared oath with another person, make sure you both understand and are comfortable with the wording.

4. As well as giving yourself time and information so you can really get to know any person or group you are sharing an oath with, also trust your own instincts about the wisdom of such an oath.

5. Think carefully about whether the oath you are planning is better served by having a time-frame, or being open-ended. A time-frame can be very helpful in some circumstances. In other circumstances, especially some kinds of relationship oaths, specifying a long-term or lifetime time-frame can cause serious problems if circumstances change and the relationship comes to an end. Some people, especially married couples, will want the strength of a lifetime commitment to give power to their oath. Other people may want to be more cautious, and keep their oath open-ended

(not specifying a length of time in the wording of the oath) to allow for changed circumstances.

6. Carefully examine any proposed oath to make sure it won't conflict with other oaths, responsibilities, commitments, and other aspects of your life.

7. Don't pile up too many demanding oaths at once; don't expect superhuman performance from yourself. As in other areas of life, realistic pacing is important for success. It is better—much, much better!—to succeed with small oaths, than to fail with big ones!

## Breaking an Oath

There are two ways that oath-breaking can happen. One is that we fail to achieve the oath, and perhaps even work against it by actions that contradict what we promised in the oath. The other way is a deliberate decision to bring an oath to an end, because changed circumstances no longer support the intent of that oath.

These two ways of oath-breaking need to be handled differently. In the case of breaking the oath through failure to fulfill it, this action has repercussions on our wyrd, luck, relationships, our might and main, our well-being and reputation. Work needs to be done to address these problems and remedy them to the extent that we can. This work is the subject of the next essay in this book: *Threads of Wyrd and Shild,* so I will not pursue it here.

Let's turn now to the subject of bringing an oath to a necessary end. If we did not specify a time-frame in the oath, then bringing it to an end does not have any severe impact on our wyrd. In the oath, a length of time for the oath to be maintained was not defined, which leaves us free to adjust to changed circumstances.

Some oaths are defined by time, either stated or strongly implied. Marriage oaths are the most common example; they are generally expected to last for a lifetime. Sometimes, sadly, this does not work out, though it may well be possible to mend the marriage by committing to the skills of oathing and other ethical skills that I describe in this book, before the marriage is completely lost.

When the marriage or other oathed commitment cannot be saved, and the original oaths must be abandoned, there are measures that can be taken to mitigate some of the harm. Perhaps the most important measure is to set up new oaths to address the harm and disruption caused by the older oath coming to an end.

In the case of divorce from a marriage that produced children, for example, the parents can commit to oaths that take the well-being of the children into account during and after the divorce has taken place. Speaking respectfully about the other parent, not pushing the children to take sides, allowing the children some choice in their circumstances if they are old enough, committing to fair and necessary financial and care arrangements that are in the best interests of the children, allowing children free access to both parents as long as no abuse was involved: all these are examples of oathed agreements that help to mitigate the impact of breaking the older oath.

Marriage and divorce are just examples. There are many other kinds of oaths and commitments that cause pain and disruption if they must be put aside. The thing to do here is to mend that situation as well as possible by putting new oaths in place, suited to the new circumstances, that can support as much good as possible in this situation.

A uniquely Heathen approach would be to add also a ceremony: a ceremony of divorce, of oath-changing, of laying an outworn oath to rest, releasing it. Such a ceremony can add strength to new, mitigating oaths if they are needed to reduce the harm and maintain what good can be maintained as circumstances change. Friendly witnesses to these ceremonies are a good thing, to support the participants as they change their lives, and as they perhaps swear new oaths of goodwill and healing. Involving others who are affected by the oath-breaking in a ceremony such as this is a way of bringing healing to all, and of re-establishing frith-bonds that were threatened by the lapse of the oath.

I hope that these guidelines will prove to be helpful and practical for you, if you decide to walk this path of Heathen might and main!

The Norns spin beneath Yggdrasil.

By L.B. Hansen, 1893

# 4. Threads of Wyrd and Shild

## A Ninefold Rite of Life Renewal

*Wounded might and main; healing personal power.*

This essay serves two purposes. One is to discuss and illustrate aspects of the workings of Wyrd and Scyld, in the context of how one might apply such knowledge in one's own life. 'Scyld' or Shild is the Anglo-Saxon equivalent of Skuld, one of the three Norns. Her name is related to 'should,' and her realm of action is 'what should be,' the consequences arising from past actions. Scyld or shild in Anglo-Saxon meant 'responsible for, liable for, in debt to,' among other meanings. The ethical meaning of 'shild' that I focus on here is 'moral debt or obligation.'

The second purpose of the essay is to provide a specific ritual based on this knowledge, which can be used to help you turn your life around, if you so choose. When you find yourself in a position where bad luck, mistakes, wrong deeds, problems of personal history, or other kinds of unhappy situations are constraining your ability to live a worthy life, this ritual can help you redesign your life and to offer a better life-thread to be woven on Wyrd's loom. Or, you may simply feel the need for a 'spiritual housecleaning' and a fresh start in your life: this ritual can also serve that purpose.

Please keep in mind that there is not enough strength in the words or ritual actions alone to effect such a change. The change must come about within yourself, affecting your understanding of and intentions toward yourself and the world around you, especially with respect to the Norns, and your own wyrd.

## The Symbolism of the Ninefold Rite

One reason the ritual provided here is called a 'Ninefold Rite' of renewal is that it is intended to reach all the different parts of our body-soul complex. The prose explanations provided in the discussion are for the sake of our conscious, rational mind, and are also meant to help strengthen and direct our will and intentionality. The 'spells' or poetic portions of the ritual are directed toward the trans-rational aspects of our souls, that deal less with logic and words, and more with imagery and symbolism, mystical consciousness, and hidden memory. The actions that are called for in the spells bring in the participation of the physical body–our lich.

Thus, with rational prose, mytho-imagic poetry, and physical action, all the parts of the body-soul complex are brought to bear in concert toward one's intention. If you can make up your own tune or chant for the spell parts of the ritual, and if you wish to add more poetry of your own composition or selection that is meaningful to you, this will further help the self-tuning and focusing process. These actions of weaving together the different parts of oneself and focusing them on one's purpose is a personal enactment or mirroring of the weaving of the manifold strands of Wyrd in the world.

The second reason this is called a 'Ninefold Rite' is because it involves three Wells, three Norns, and three steps. The Wells are the *Well of Wyrd, Mimir's Well,* and *Hvergelmir.*

The *Well of Wyrd* holds the pattern of That-Which-Is, created by the strands of all significant deeds and events that have occurred, including your own: the orlay (Anglo-Saxon) or ørlög (Old Norse) you have laid in the Well. All that is now coming into being is influenced by the pattern of Wyrd that has already been laid. To change the influence of Wyrd for the better, it is necessary for you to add another deed–a life-changing deed and a deed of might–to this pattern, which will hopefully help to turn That-Which-Is-Becoming in a better direction for you. What has been woven in the past cannot be erased, but what is woven in the present can catch up the threads dangling from the past and weave them into a new pattern.

*Mimir's Well* is the collective memory of all the folk– the collective unconscious, to use another frame of reference. It contains all wisdom, knowledge and memory that have been. Woden's eye lies in this Well, the price for his draught of wisdom from it. People go to this well to seek wisdom and understanding, and in turn, wisdom, memory and understanding that we gain during the course of our lives eventually finds its way into the treasure-hoard of Mimir's Well. Gaining even a small amount of wisdom and transpersonal memory from Mimir's Well often allows one to better understand and interpret the events and conditions of one's life, and casts the whole pattern of it into a clearer perspective.

*Hvergelmir*, meaning 'the roaring cauldron,' is the churning cauldron, the whirling source of the great Wells: a mighty entity that is beyond any close-up human perception and knowledge. I believe, myself, that the whelming and stirring of this well is powered by the perpetual creative force that occurs when the primal Ice and Fire meet in Ginnungagap—the chasm of unbeing within which the worlds are born. I think that Hvergelmir can be a source of randomness, newness and change, that can sometimes appear and surge up through the other Wells, subtly affecting their contents and patterns.

## Shild and the Actions of the Norns

*Wyrd* or *Urdh* is the Norn who rules the Well of Wyrd and That-Which-Is, creating a pattern out of all our deeds and events that shapes the process of becoming. *Werthende* (WARE-then-deh) or *Verðandi* is the Norn who presides over That-Which-Is-Becoming, the very instant when a being or a deed comes into existence. *Scyld* or *Skuld* spins the thread that is formed from the 'shild,' the moral debt or obligation, that we incur by our choices, commitments and deeds or lack thereof, in our lives, current and past, and sometimes indirectly from the lives of any whose wyrd has been woven together with ours through kinship or oath bonds. I use 'Scyld' to refer to the Norn, and 'shild' to refer to moral debt, though they are the same word.

The shild we incur can be of a positive nature, something we have earned by our efforts, as would be contained in the main (soul-power) and the luck that are generated by an oath given and kept or a good deed done. Or, it can be of a negative nature, such as the moral debt (including loss of main—soul power—and luck) generated by an oath forsworn or an ill deed done. This essay will primarily focus on the effects of negative shild, or moral debt. Some of the workings, effects and benefits of positive shild, leading to stronger mains and good wyrd, are discussed in my previous two essays about Oaths.

Shild-threads are attached to any deed, action, or being that arises in the moment of Becoming, and again at any time during their span of existence that the being, deed, or action generates shild. Through these threads, Scyld tugs upon that deed or being, affecting their path and outcome, according to the shild that has accumulated from their past. More shild may be added, strengthening the thread, as the being or the deed continues its existence and effects.

Looking at this effect from the outside, it may seem to us that Scyld is 'the future,' inevitable and set, but this is not necessarily the case. It is often possible to pay at least some of our negative shild in some way, which then reduces the strength of the shild-thread that tugs at our wyrd, leaving us with more freedom of choice for our future directions.

Thus, if we hope to create a change in our wyrd, we must first settle any shild–any moral debt or obligation–that our deeds or lack of deeds may have brought about. Or, it may be that we have made an oath, promise or commitment, that has not been fulfilled, and which we can now determine to fulfill. When this has been done, there is a greater degree of freedom, an opportunity, that opens up out of the pattern of That-Which-Is, just as it is shading into That-Which-Is-Becoming.

If there are no threads of shild, or fewer, thinner ones, attached to this new Becoming, it is more free to move in a different direction, according to one's will. This degree of freedom that comes about, seized with true-hearted intent and strength of soul, offers a chance to turn one's wyrd toward the better.

It is not complete freedom or randomness, indeed: all that comes about is shaped by the patterns of Wyrd that have already been laid, and this pattern cannot be torn out or uprooted. But the beginnings of a new pattern can often be woven onto the tail-ends of the old pattern, if one has the insight and determination to go about it rightly. The steps of the ritual described here are intended to help guide one in this process.

## 'Turning'

You will notice that in the final part of the spell associated with each step is the process of 'turning.' There is deep meaning associated with this process. The word *wyrd* itself is derived from an ancient Germanic word meaning 'to turn, to wind.' In a rite of renewal, what one wishes to do is turn away from the old, negative patterns and ways, and turn toward a new and better path. Spinning–the process of turning, twisting, winding raw fiber into thread–is one of the mightiest deeds of power and magic recognized by our Heathen forebears. Spinning was thought to influence wyrd itself. Even today, many folktales survive in which a spindle and / or thread plays a fateful role in the story, or appears in the tale as an indicator that mighty magic or mystery is about to occur.

The inclusion of the 'turning verse' in each spell of this ritual is intended to align you with this mystery of turning, of winding wyrd. If you can, physically perform the action of turning around as you speak or chant the verse, holding in your focused mind a perception of the 'power of turning' on all the planes of existence as you do so.

Imagine yourself as a spindle, and hold the image of the Tree itself: the Spindle of Wyrd, the Axis of the Worlds, around which they turn and have their being. You may continue to repeat the turning verse, until you feel that the stated intention of the verse has been brought about. (It is advisable to turn around slowly, however, to avoid dizziness! Alternatively, make these turns in your imagination.) If you have the skill, you could use a distaff and spindle to spin thread instead, as you chant the turning verses.

## Step One: Forming Your Intent

It is best to act out each of these steps to the extent possible. Try to find a body of water, a hole in the ground, a cave, a cliffside, or some other location that could symbolize the Wells for this step. If you have to, dig a hole yourself, or find some other creative alternative.

Before you begin the rite, braid, spin or twist for yourself a cord or thread in colors that symbolize for you what it is you want to change or overcome in your life.

If you do not have access to any of these things, work with images of them in your imagination, or find simple objects or locations that can symbolize these things for you. For example, a circle drawn on a piece of paper, or a cup or bowl, can symbolize a Well. A sock can stand in place of a cord, if you have no access to string or thread. Anything that you decide is your chosen symbol will work for you in this ritual.

The thing you want to change through this ritual could be one or more deeds you did that were wrong or badly mistaken, a negative attitude, a run of bad luck, failure or neglect of some obligation or duty, some part of yourself that has developed in undesirable ways even if that was not all your own doing, or whatever else is wrong.

As you braid or twist your cord (or wring and twist your sock-cord!), put into the cord all the feelings and consequences that arise from the aspect you are trying to change. Chant over your cord, shout at it (in private!), cry tears on it, grind it in your teeth, tie it in knots, stomp on it, carry it around with you and live with it for awhile, do a rune-working with it. Do whatever you need to, to make sure you've really inserted the negative energy you're trying to change, into the cord! This is no longer just a plain old string, but something a good deal more.

If you are going to throw this cord into a body of water or other natural area, choose something natural or biodegradable to make your cord out of. For example: twisted grass or thin flexible twigs, seaweed, bread dough twisted and baked, taffy that you make, stretch and twist yourself. These materials may not stand up to all of the rough treatment I suggest above, but some creative thought will lead you to other options. For example, you could keep your bread dough in the refrigerator for several days and take it out from time to time to pound and knead your feelings into it, before you bake it.

As you begin the rite, go to the place you have chosen at a time that is meaningful to you. Enact the rite by holding the cord tightly in one hand, then pulling it out slowly with difficulty and force, using your other hand. If your 'cord' is of delicate material, pull more gently but tense your muscles hard to make your body feel the work, like isotonic exercise. Take as long as you need, repeating the verse and / or adding more poetry or your own words to it, to visualize and feel this drawing-out from yourself of the aspects you want to change. If there is pain, anger, or other ill feelings associated with the drawing-out process, allow yourself to feel them fully. Then throw the cord into the water, hole, bowl, circle, or wherever you have chosen, representing Hvergelmir.

Then as you chant the words aloud, envision the transformation of this thread as it passes through the Wells: its unraveling and unwinding in the violent churning of Hvergelmir, then the shredded strands floating up from Hvergelmir into Mimir's quiet cavern-well, there to combine with strands of wisdom and memory from the past, and begin to reassemble itself into a new configuration.

51

If you are scientifically inclined, you can envision this as sort of a metaphysical 'recombinant DNA' process, with the shredded strands representing bits of DNA from an outworn chromosome, the wisdom and memory from Mimir's Well as the genes that guide the re-assembly, and the new configuration being a new chromosome with different characteristics, that will guide the development of new soul-qualities in you!

Pause as long as you wish between the phrases of the spell, to meditate on the images that come to mind. When you come to the turning-chant, physically turn yourself around. ('Hvergelmir' is pronounced *VAIR-gel-meer,* with a hard 'g', and with the addition of a strong, huffing H-sound at the beginning. Or if it is hard to say that way, you can leave the 'H' off.) Repeat the spell as many times as you wish, perhaps with the addition of other poetic lines of your choice, until you feel a sense of completion and closure for this step of the rite.

Words to speak or chant:

*Pull out and cast off cursed woe-working threads,*
*Thrown to Hvergelmir's spinning deeps:*

*Whelmed....*

*Torn asunder.....*

*Re-spun....*

52

*New-shaped to ripple and shimmer*
*Through Mimir's moss-cool cavern,*
*Through World-Mind's echoing dimness,*
*Spinning new wisdom out of ancient strands.*

*Turn and turn again,*
*Turn and turn again,*
*Bind off old threads*
*Wind and weave anew.*

If the place you have thrown your cord is not a place that will 'take it away' the way a river or the ocean would do, or a hole in the ground that you can bury, then first dry the cord if it is wet, and afterwards burn it in a fireproof container. If you cannot do that, then 'decommission' your cord / sock / whatever, by declaring that it has served its purpose and now is no longer your symbol. Put it aside, unused, for as long as you can, so its symbolic force can dissipate.

## Step Two: Paying Your Shild

This step must be taken with the utmost seriousness, taking all the time you need to do it right. It could take weeks, months, or more, if your shild is heavy. Even if the thing that is wrong, that you are trying to change, seems not to be your fault or not entirely your fault, it is still important to look for traces of shild, from this life, past lives, or from the orlay of your kin.

The paying of shild is in part the great deed you will do, to repattern the weavings of wyrd in your life. (The other part of the deed is your firm intention to change your life, and then doing it.) Try to stand outside yourself, looking at the situation objectively so that you place neither too much nor too little responsibility on yourself for the thing you are trying to change. If you have a wise and trusted friend who is not too closely involved in the situation, you might seek this person's rede to make sure you are taking a well-balanced view of the circumstances.

### *Examining your shild*

Meditate on the situation, letting your mind roam back to the roots of what has happened in your life, and follow those threads through your life until you understand at least the basic nature of the causes-and-effects that brought you where you are. Mentally placing yourself in Mimir's cavern as you do this, seated next to his dark well, may help to infuse ancient wisdom and the knowledge of your forebears in your process of life-examination. You may also wish to make an offering to the Norns, Mimir, and/or to any of our Goddesses or Gods whom you think could best help you do this well, and ask their aid: their clear sight and fair judgement to guide you.

Two runes can be of special help in your efforts here: Nauthiz or 'Need,' and Fehu or 'Fee.' Strive to recognize the shape and nature of what is needed, and what fee would balance or redress that need. *Fee often can balance need:* this is the principle that lies behind *wergild*–the fee paid for damages done to person or property, or even to one's dignity in some cases. This principle in fact goes much deeper into the metaphysical realms, having to do with the balance of *hamingja,* or spiritual power and luck, between persons and other beings and processes, and how injury, damage or insult throws the balance off.

Wergild, in the past, was not intended as a punishment *per se,* but rather as a way to redress an imbalance in how hamingja and luck were distributed between one person and another, caused by their deeds and injuries. This is why our forebears generally required wergild regardless of whether the injury was caused deliberately or accidentally, or even completely unknowingly. Fault, blame, and punishment were not the basic issue, nor the primary reason for requiring wergild, at least not during Heathen times. Rather, wergild was intended to right the imbalance of spiritual power–and also the dishonor–caused by the injury, however that injury came about.

The more humane and less socially-disruptive concept of wergild gradually replaced the older idea that blood-vengeance, not payment, was the only way to redress such an imbalance– although staunch, old-style Heathens such as Egil Skallagrimson steadily and scornfully dismissed the idea that wergild could ever suffice in place of blood-vengeance! (Any detailed discussion of these principles is somewhat beyond the scope of this essay. The chapters on Honor, and Vengeance, in Volume I of Vilhelm Grønbech's *Culture of the Teutons,* offer a good discussion of this whole concept.)

In our own lives, if the fee owed is not honored, if shild is not acknowledged and addressed, then the heavy weight of need generated by shild can throw the whole pattern of one's wyrd out of kilter, causing many distressing effects in one's life.

## *Going deeper*

Use the words of the rite (given on page 61) to focus your meditation and thought, until it becomes clear to you whether you have any unmet obligations, or whether any shild is owed, and if so what an appropriate wergild or payment of the shild would be. Usually, the best form in which to make the payment is one which is as much like the cause of the shild as possible (though you may wish to multiply your fee severalfold greater than the shild you perceive, in accordance with the Heathen thew or virtue of generosity).

For example, if you caused someone to lose something they valued (material or non-material), try to find something to give them that they will value as much as, or preferably more than, that which they lost. If you harmed someone–whether intentionally or not (you still have responsibility, even if you do not have 'fault 'or 'blame,'), then find some way to be of service to them or to someone else who could represent them.

You cannot always reach the one who was harmed, and may sometimes need to find a logical substitute. For example, if you harmed or neglected a child who is now grown or is unreachable, then do something good for another child. If bad luck which has been plaguing you has made the world seem an ugly place, create beauty in some way that will bring joy to others–to humans and/or other beings such as landwights or housewights. (Not uncommonly, 'bad luck' can be caused by offending or neglecting some of the other beings who inhabit the worlds with us, but whose presence is often not obvious to us.)

It is not always possible to make up for some harm you did to the same person or entity to whom you caused the harm. This is especially true if the shild attached to your life was originally generated by some ill-fated pattern in your family line, that might go back many generations. For example, some of my family's genealogical research indicates that I might be descended from the 8th century emperor Charlemagne. As was pointed out to me by one Heathen, only half-jokingly, it may take the efforts of a good number of Heathen generations of Charlemagne's offspring, to repay or rebalance the enormous shild he earned for his family line by his oppressive treatment of Heathen folk during his lifetime!

As a more modern example, it is unfortunately all too easy to find ill-fated, shild-generating patterns running through a family line, such as generation after generation of spouse or child abusers, as well as less lurid but still harmful patterns such as selfishness and neglect of one's proper obligations in life.

Thus, it may be that the shild that is unbalancing your life was not even earned by you, or not entirely by you, in addition to the fact that you may not be able to reach whoever was harmed in order to repay them. And, easily enough, if the shild is something that runs in your family line, you may well have been the recipient of harm yourself, in addition to owning your share of the family shild for harm done to others.

This seems a bit unfair, on first glance, does it not? Sort of a double-whammy situation, a nasty tangle of wyrd- and shild-threads. Yet there is no denying that–fault or no fault– if this is indeed the case then this load of shild is a burden on your life and your wyrd. It should be addressed with courage and determination, in order to make room for a new and better strand to be cast onto the loom of Wyrd to improve your lot and that of the generations to come after you.

## *Restitution*

If you yourself suffered harm for which you also own some of the kin-shild, try to find another family member for whom you could do something good–especially a child, for whom you might try to break or mitigate the family pattern of ill before it is ingrained in the child. (It is also easier not to blame a child for any kin-grudges that you might hold, in contrast to dealing with older members of the family.) Regard this relative whom you are benefiting as being a substitute for yourself, when you were harmed in the past. This way, your chosen substitute will be gaining payment for the injury done to you, at the same time that you are paying off your share of the kin-shild, thus evening out two harmful imbalances in one fell swoop!

Rest assured that this would be an authentically traditional Heathen way of dealing with your dilemma, if you have such a dilemma. Elder Heathens regularly acted on the assumption that kinfolk were very acceptable substitutes for each other when it came to vengeance, paying or accepting wergild, erasing dishonor, and other ways of rebalancing their situation.

This makes it very clear that they did not regard wergild, or even vengeance, as being 'punishment.' What would be the point of punishing someone who did not even commit the ill deed–who perhaps was totally unaware of it, or even tried to prevent it? But since kinfolk could stand for each other, then when they were trying to rebalance the situation–the loss of *hamingja*, other forms of luck, and honor –one kinsman was as good as another. It did not really matter who paid, as long as somebody did. And–bottom line in terms of Heathen belief–one way or another, Scyld received her due if this was done: balance was restored and the shild did not hang on and on to plague everybody.

If it is not possible to work in this way with your literal kin, you can 'adopt' someone informally, someone in need of your help, and work with this person to pay your shild through help and service. Likewise, you could work on behalf of a group or a cause, such as a charity. Or simply do something for your 'neighbor'—anyone who is available to you: offer help, support, understanding, a listening ear, acts of simple kindness.

So, what you are seeking to do in this step of the ritual is rebalance something that is out of balance, out of kilter: rebalance 'you' with 'the world' so you are in right relationship with the world again. This needs to be done whether the lack of balance seems to be your fault or not, or even if it is not clear whose fault it is, or whether it is anyone's fault. Even if you cannot figure out the cause and effect, or who owns the obvious responsibility for the situation, usually an act of rebalancing will address the problem.

If after all your careful thought and meditation, you still seem to have no reason to pay anyone anything as wergild, then make a gift to the world out of sheer Heathen generosity. Imagine that you are sitting on one side of a balance-scale. What should go in the dish on the other side of the scale, to 'balance' you? Try out various gifts to see which one looks or feels right in your imagination. A gift could be a deed of service, a donation or contribution, a work of your own craft or art, some gesture of generosity of spirit. It could be given to someone close to you, or to a needy stranger, to the environment or the landwights, to your community, to one God or Goddess or to all of them....the possibilities are endless!

## The Shild-Rite

Seek and use the inner core of your healthiest instincts, your inner sense of rightness, to decide what is the best gift or wergild to give. You may want to make use of some art of divination, such as rune casting or spaeworking, to help you seek this knowledge. You can use the first two verses of the following spell to help you focus your meditation and determination on this work, repeating them as long as needed, and adding more to the verses if you wish. Then, repeat them together with the last verse (the turning spell) a final time, to mark your deed when the work of this step is done. If you complete this step of shild-knowing and shild-paying, truly you will have done a great deed to mark and honor, worthy of a song!

*Seek now to know what's owed;*
*Scyld's rede lies deep and cold.*
*Nor think to stint her meed:*
*Give fee to balance need.*

*All wergild find*
*In coin or kind:*
*Scyld cleanses heart and mind.*

*Turn and turn again,*
*Turn and turn again,*
*So Scyld is paid her due:*
*Now wind and weave anew.*

*(Note: The word 'stint' in this sense means to give ungenerously, to hold back in your giving. 'Meed' means something that is deserved or earned, a person's rightful share. 'Coin or kind' is an old phrase that means 'you can pay me with money, or with barter or service.' 'Scyld' is pronounced 'Shild.')*

## Step Three: Weaving Anew

Now you have cleared the decks of your life, to the extent you can do so: you have consciously sought an understanding of your wyrd, and have addressed to the best of your ability any shild that might be owing. These actions certainly do not erase your wyrd as a whole–one would not wish this to happen in any case. To be wyrdless is simply not to exist as a conscious, responsible being. But your actions have helped to 'clean out the closet,' so to speak, and make room for some new, brighter threads to be cast onto the loom of Wyrd.

Be aware that these new threads will of course become a part of your wyrd, so think carefully about your new directions and choices, seeking always the most honorable and virtuous path according to Heathen thew (virtues and values). It is helpful to open your mind to godly guidance through meditation and perhaps an offering, and you could again make use of some form of divination, to give you indications for good choices. Your struggle, your effort to change your life, is itself a deed–a mighty one–laid in the Well or cast onto the loom to affect your wyrd. This deed of change should itself be done rightly and truly, as the first of the new and better threads to be attached to your wyrd.

Werthende or Verðandi, as the Norn of Becoming, helps shape your present actions and decisions, and her help and blessing should be sought–perhaps with an offering, certainly with your acknowledgement and thanks. Scyld or Skuld has helped you, in her often painful way, by forcing you to clean out and rebalance that which needed such action.

Though dealing with these requirements is not pleasant, it is necessary to do so. Keeping the fibers of the multiverse well-strung, taut and properly balanced, is Scyld's task. Difficult though we might find the experience as individuals, the well-being of the multiverse as a whole depends on her actions of balancing, of getting the tensions just right. As you lay the new strands of your worthy deeds into the hands of the Norns, ask Wyrd herself to take them up and weave them into the fabric of That-Which-Is, continuing the process of wyrd and of life.

As your final act, now braid, spin or twist a new cord, symbolizing the new strand of wyrd that you want to attach to your life-patterns. Speak or chant the first verse of the final spell as you wind this new cord, pausing to meditate as needed:

*New patterns out of ancient Wyrd-might flow;*
*On darker web, now weave a brighter hue.*
*From pain and struggle bring forth a new birth—*
*Bid Werthende's blessing on the new strand's worth.*

Then, place the cord into a bowl of water. If possible, the bowl should be beautiful and/ or of special meaning to you–perhaps an heirloom of your family or a gift from someone you care about. You might wish to draw the water from a stream, lake or well, if one is available. Place the cord in the bowl as you begin the second part of the spell, meditating on the actions of the Wells. If you are not able to do these things, use whatever you can, and envision the Well in your imagination.

Pause for as long as you wish between the phrases, or repeat them, to let the meanings and images sink in. Feel deep in yourself the strength of your intention to turn your life around, fed by the power of the Wells, as you reach in and draw forth your cord: washed, blessed, and charged with the might of the Wells. Then, perform your final turnings, turning toward a new and better wyrd and pattern for your life.

*Three Wells draw in*
*Three Wells flow out*
*Shaping mighty deeds of worth.*
*Now: bring true honor forth!*

*Turn and turn again,*
*Turn and turn again,*
*Ever old and ever new:*
*In Wyrd, all deeds come due.*

Know that your new deeds, deeds of Heathen worth, are likely to be taken up by Wyrd and woven into the pattern of all that is, creating a new and better wyrd for you and for those whose lives you touch. Save the cord you have wound in some honored place–perhaps on your harrow–to remind you of your new path of life. As you close your rite of renewal, give honor from your heart and soul to the great Wells, to Mimir and the Norns: embodiments of the processes of existence itself. It is no small thing to try to deal directly with these powers. As Heathens, we are fortunate to have ways to grasp and communicate some understanding of these patterns and powers, and have the might of soul to be able to work with them to better our own lot.

# 5. Heathen Frith and Modern Ideals

*Interwoven might and main:*
*The roots of relationship and community.*

*Frith* is often translated as 'peace'. The full meaning of frith encompasses peace but extends well beyond it, to cover a large portion of the most meaningful and essential foundations of human social life. A full understanding of the concept of frith will show that 'peace' is not identical to frith; rather, peace is generally an *outgrowth* of frith, resulting from the conditions of frith being met. When frith has been achieved, usually peace is there too, though that is not always the case, as I shall show.

Here I will summarize the ancient roots of frith, and then go on to write about a newer source of frith in the modern world: a shared loyalty towards ideals and principles, as distinct from ancient Heathen loyalty to kin and lord. The other matter I will address here is that frith, while an excellent thing, like all human endeavors has its own pitfalls. Awareness of these pitfalls allows us to avoid or work around them, rather than being unwittingly sucked into them. The two main pitfalls that I discuss here concern the dynamics of group behavior, and some dilemmas relating to tolerance of differences.

Earlier Germanic peoples perceived three primary focuses or centers of frith. The first—and surely the original—wellspring of frith was kinship and kindreds. The second was the web of loyalty created among a leader, lord or chieftain and his (occasionally her) folk. The third wellspring of frith arose from the relationships between the folk and their Gods, Goddesses and other holy wights, as well as between individuals of the folk who had come together in the presence of their Deities. (I am indebted to Vilhelm Grønbech's volumes on *The Culture of the Teutons* for parts of these discussions on ancient frith.)

## Frith and Kinship

The idea of frith is very closely tied to kinship—blood kinship in particular—and then to kinship by marriage, adoption and fostering. The words *frith* and *sib* were often used interchangeably to describe the state of people involved in a kindred relationship, and we can easily see the connection in the modern use of the term *sibling* to indicate a brother or sister. The term *frith* did not merely indicate the material fact of blood relationship. Rather, it described the essence of the relationship itself: the joys, responsibilities, interdependence, burdens, and benefits that characterized it.

The word frith is related to the words for *friend* and *free*. Frith was to our forebears the "power that makes them 'friends' towards one another, and free men towards the rest of the world." *(Grønbech, Vol. I, p. 32.)* In their minds, 'freedom' did not mean freedom from responsibility toward others. 'Freedom' meant being strong enough to face the ill-happenings of the world and being able to overcome or survive them. For this, one depended on one's kindred.

Surrounded by a numerous kindred cognizant of the requirements of frith, the Germanic man or woman was well-armored against many misfortunes the world could cast, whether poverty, threats of violence, legal troubles, or other difficulties. Not woven into a web of frith, the lonely wretch had nothing either material or spiritual upon which to rest life and welfare. This also was the bitter lot of thralls.

One can read again and again in the Icelandic Sagas of a worthless, trouble-making person whose actions bring disgrace and disaster on the whole kindred, but who, nevertheless, is supported, helped and defended by other members of the kindred who are committed to upholding frith no matter what the consequences. Grønbech notes the "absolute character of frith, its freedom from all reservation"*(Vol. I, p. 36)*. This absolute, uncompromising character of kindred-oriented frith actually contributed significantly to the pursuit of feuds and strife within the larger community, at the same time that it reduced strife within the kindred, inside the pale of frith.

Frith was nothing if not partisan: focused on security and stability of the kindred, it had no application to those individuals and groups who lay outside the boundaries when it came to a conflict of interest between them. Nor could any notion of absolute, unbiased justice make a dent in it: defending one's kindred was always right, no matter how wrong their actions were. Frith was the paramount virtue, taking precedence over all others.

Often women, as brides, were meant to serve as frithweavers between warring clans. When, as too often happened, the frith thus woven broke down, the effect on women of the conflict between loyalty to lord (husband) versus kin was severe. As far as I am aware, though, there seems to have been no question in our forebears' minds that a woman's loyalty belonged first to her kin. Gudrun of the *Volsunga Saga* is a perfect example: she could not allow herself to take vengeance on her brothers for their murder of her husband Sigurd, in spite of her bitter grief at his death. Though she loved her husband dearly, that love could not outweigh the demands of kin-frith. Yet she had no hesitation enacting vengeance on her next husband, the Hun leader Atli, for her brothers' deaths. This was done in order to keep frith—kin-frith—whole.

Women indeed acted as peace weavers, not only within the kindred but also in the community, and inspiring examples of their deeds can be found in the literature. The same, of course, can be said for many men. Yet women sometimes acted against peace, as we would see it today, by being the keepers of the family frith and honor, and ensuring that vengeance was taken when one of their own had been injured. The Icelandic and Germanic Sagas give many instances of women who prodded their more peaceable or just lazy or feckless (in the mindset of the times) menfolk into taking vengeance when the men perhaps would not have chosen to do so, if they had been left alone.

This clearly illustrates some of the underlying differences between the concept of *frith,* and the modern idea of *peace*—a word which is often used to translate 'frith.' Elder folk regarded the courageous act of marrying into an enemy clan as frithweaving, which we would indeed regard as 'peace weaving' today. But they also saw vengeance against those who broke through the boundaries of frith—outsiders who damaged their kindred in some way—as being properly supportive of frith. This willingness to take vengeance would not be described as 'peaceful' behavior today!

## The Bond between Leaders and Folk

Due most likely to the violent, insecure and threatening world in which they lived, Germanic peoples in many, though not all, places and times of their history laid great emphasis on a close and loyal relationship between leader and folk. This reached its highest expression in the oathed relationship between a war leader and war band, though it also applied to peacetime chieftains, kings and other leaders. This relationship between lord and sworn man was frequently extolled in the heroic poetry and sagas of the age, so that we have good records of what it ideally involved.

Frith between lord and man was expressed much as the frith of kinship: there were mutual obligations and benefits, including the requirement for the man not to raise hand or voice against his lord, and the lord not to punish or deprive his man and the man's dependents unjustly. In essence, the lord owed the man his livelihood, while the man owed the lord his life and service. Under the social conditions present in those times, neither could survive safely or comfortably without the other; thus the importance of making and maintaining bonds of trust and frith between them. This was often strengthened by the fact that there were kin relationships within these groups, also. This gave a double foundation for frith: it was both oath-bound and kinship-bound.

The men sworn to a lord were likewise expected to keep peace and trust among themselves. Anglo-Saxon literature is rich in references to the *healldream*, the 'joys of the hall,' where the deep frith between members of a war band or other oathed group, seated blithely in the lord's hall, closely matched the gladness and security ideally available within the homes of families and kindreds.

The strong attachment to a lord could, on occasion, create a conflict between kinship-frith and oath-frith. For example, the *Anglo-Saxon Chronicle* entry for the year 755 C.E. has a complicated account of fighting between Cynewulf and Cyneheard. Cynewulf attacked and killed Cyneheard; Cyneheard's thanes were determined to protect his body and avenge him. When these thanes were offered money and safe-conduct by kinsmen who were in the opposing force, they answered that "no kinsman was dearer to them than their lord, and they would never follow his slayer." The *Laws of Alfred* (late 800's) state that a lord and his follower may each fight on each other's behalf without penalty of law, and a man may so fight on behalf of a blood relative, but a man "may not take the side of a kinsman against his lord—that we do not permit." *(Griffiths p. 73-74)*

It appears that among the Anglo-Saxons and most likely their continental Germanic forebears, the oathed frith-relationship between lord and sworn man stood highest of all values, while among the Icelanders and their Scandinavian forebears, the frith of kinship was paramount. This difference had, I believe, complex implications regarding the extent of feuding, strife and litigation present within the larger communities of these two cultural groups (Icelandic and Anglo-Saxon), but this is a large topic outside the scope of this essay.

## Frith between Folk and the Holy Ones

Frithful behavior was a highly important sign of respect and troth on the part of ancient Heathens toward their Gods, Goddesses, land-wights, and their ancestral Disir and Alfar. This is attested to by the prevalence of 'frithyards' and frithsteads found everywhere that Germanic peoples settled, and often mentioned in the literature of the time. Frithyards were enclosures or areas of land, including those around temples and outdoor harrows or altars, where all present were required to keep frith in the sense of abstaining from violence and from instigating violence by uncivil behavior.

Frithyards were to be kept holy in several respects, the primary one being that no bloodshed, fighting or severe quarreling were allowed. One well-known example of the required behavior in a frithyard is given in *Eyrbyggja Saga*, Chapter 4, about the Thor's-Godhi Thorolf Mostur-Beard and his holy mountain Helgafell. Things (assemblies) were held at the foot of the mountain, at the place where Thorolf's Thor's-pillar had first come to land. No bloodshed nor excrement were allowed in the area—folk had to go off to a rock in the sea to relieve themselves! (Indeed, the very term used for 'to relieve oneself' meant literally 'to go drive out the

71

alfs.') Chapter 9 of the same Saga tells of the deliberate desecration of the frithstead by the Kjallekling clan, and the resulting bloodshed as Thorolf's kin tried to defend the land they regarded as holy.

Again, as we see in the context of kin-frith and oath-frith, the establishment and defense of frithsteads holy to the Gods could also result in violence and death. As an interesting aside, the fight over Thorolf's frithstead was finally broken up by a team of respected peacemakers who, when they were at first unsuccessful, threatened to join the fighting on the side of whichever clan first agreed to listen to them. This immediately broke up the fight. Something to keep in mind, perhaps!

Both temporary and permanent frithsteads were used by ancient Heathens. Temporary frithsteads were usually the Thingsteads or places of assembly: meeting-places. Frith was kept there both to honor the Deities and as a practical matter, in that the business of the Thing could not properly be conducted if frith were not maintained. Permanent frithsteads, often called frithyards, were generally associated with a temple, shrine, or other holy spot such as a well or a sacred tree, or a boulder housing a local landwight. Frithyards were holy not only to major Deities, but also and perhaps even more commonly, to 'minor' holy wights such as landwights, well-wights, or family forebears (Disir and Alfar).

Holy beings, both high and low, for the most part love frith and demand it from their followers and their human neighbors. Landwights, well-wights, woodwives, housewights, and most other beneficial nature spirits dislike strife, as is shown in many folktales of the Germanic peoples. They tend to leave their steads, taking their main, luck, and hamingja with them, if subjected to too much strife, bloodshed, or lack of respect on the part of quarrelsome or greedy humans. They will also leave if they feel betrayed by their human friends and neighbors, showing that frith comprises not only absence of strife, but also ties of loyalty. (On this subject, see also the section on *Guardian Spirits* in Davidson.)

The central importance of frithyards to Heathen worship is exemplified by the fact that centuries after Germanic countries were supposedly Christianized, kings and church leaders still found it necessary to promulgate strict laws and penalties against having and visiting 'peace enclosures' (frithyards) on one's own property or anywhere else. One example is the *16th Canon Law* enacted under England's King Edgar (939-946), some 300 years into the period of Christian dominance: "And we enjoin that every priest...totally extinguish every heathenism, and forbid well-worshiping, and spiritualism, and divinations, and enchantments, and idol-worshiping, and the vain practices which are carried on with various spells, *and with peace-enclosures,* and with elders (the tree), and also with various other trees, and with stones...." *(Linsell, p. 161.).*

The main point to be made here is that the frithstead or frithyard was not only intended to be a place where peace was enforced. It was also a reminder and a commitment to the fact that Heathen folk are in a relationship with their

Deities and friendly spirits: a relationship of frith, that involves trust, respect, mutual benefit, and mutual obligation, including but not limited to behaving in a peaceful manner toward one another.

## The Role of Frith in Religious Conversion

An intriguing question asked by sociologists of religion is this: what conditions make people receptive or unreceptive to the message of a new religion? Why do some people willingly convert, while others resist to the death? Clearly, there are many factors involved in the complex phenomena of religious conversion and resistance to conversion, but one very important factor is the frith or lack thereof existing in a society at the time that conversion is attempted. (This section, in part, summarizes the findings of an excellent book, *The Germanization of Early Medieval Christianity: A Sociohistorical Approach to Religious Transformation,* by James C. Russell.)

In the Mediterranean cultures at the beginning of the Christian era, the expansion and then the social decline of the Roman Empire brought about huge areas of cultural decay. People of many cultures within the Roman Empire had been uprooted from their places, religions, social structures and social status as a result of imposing and maintaining the Imperium. Slavery and serfdom, poverty, helplessness and hopelessness were widespread. These people had no bonds of frith to sustain them; they were adrift in a sea of meaninglessness and helplessness.

In these circumstances, the Christian message of universal love and salvation was welcome to many people who felt disempowered and worthless in the overall scheme of things. The new religion gave their lives meaning and purpose, and gave them a sense of place in the world. The Christian churches welcomed them regardless of their social status, and gave them a real frithstead to replace their rootlessness. There was no need, at the beginning, for Christians to pursue forcible conversion since their message was a powerful one among a good number of people in that time and place.

Some centuries later, as the Christians of the Middle Sea cultures attempted to extend their message northward into the rest of Europe, the picture was a very different one. Instead of rootless people whose culture and sense of self-worth had been eroded by conditions in the Empire, Christian missionaries faced people who were solidly rooted in the social contexts of pagan Indo-European frith relationships. The message of 'salvation' was not very impressive when Heathens did not feel they really needed to be saved from anything by some foreigner who stood outside their own webs of frith and troth. Any 'salvation' needed – and this would have been interpreted in very practical, mundane ways like overcoming their opponents – could be supplied by their own kindreds, leaders, social structures, and their own Holy Ones.

The message of universal love and acceptance was likewise less than impressive, when compared to the strength and reliability of the age-old frith structures in which these people were imbedded. Charity, the support of orphans and widows, generosity to the stranger and the poor? These values were already present in Heathen culture, though surely not always practiced as they should have been. A place to belong, the knowledge that you are reliably supported by others both human and divine, and owe them your support in turn? This is Heathen frith; they did not need Christians to teach them about this.

In a nutshell, the Christian message of personal salvation—so powerful when offered to rootless, unconnected, helpless individuals—seemed unimpressive and pointless to most Germanic Heathens, as long as they retained their traditional structures of frith. In the face of such ingrained resistance, such a different philosophy and world-view as they faced among the Germanic peoples, the Christian missionaries and their political backers had to resort to political, economic, military, legal, and physical coercion, along with skillful spin-doctoring and obfuscation, in order to forcibly convert these people. The basic message of Russell's book is that all of the accommodations, spin-doctoring, and other efforts that Christians had to make, in order to make Christianity appealing and comprehensible to the Germanic peoples, actually backfired and resulted just as much in Christianity being 'Germanized' as in Germanic peoples being 'Christianized.'

The Christianity that came out at the other end of the Germanic Christianization process bore, in many ways, little resemblance to the Middle Sea Christianity that went into it at the beginning. The legacy of this outcome resulted in many Christian schisms and struggles, extending to the present day, as Christians tried to figure out and return to 'true' (i.e. pre-Germanic pagan) Christianity. Ironically, by undermining and redirecting pagan Germanic frith, Christians introduced more seeds of unfrithfulness within their own structure.

A crucial factor in this resilience and resistance to conversion on the part of Germanic culture was their strength of frith in the overall scheme of things. People simply cannot survive and thrive without frith, the fabric of family and society: neither physically, socially, emotionally nor spiritually. A person who lacks any context of frith in their life, the lost and seeking person, will give all their loyalty to the ones who offer them a structure of frith. Here lies the appeal of any cult or any religion, including ours, which will offer a home of the heart to those who seek.

## From Elder Days to Today

Thus we have seen that the ancient concept of frith was powerful and deep among our elder kin, and was based upon three fundamental roots: kinship, the loyal commitments between leaders and folk, and the relationship between folk and the Holy Ones.

After conversion of the Germanic peoples to Christianity, a hybrid form of frith arose that was expressed during the Middle Ages as militant Christianity. The Heathen frith-loyalty between lord and sworn warrior was transformed into frith-loyalty of warriors and knights to the Christian God as directed by the Church, to whom they swore their lives and service. This resulted in the various Crusades and the Inquisition, where Muslims, Pagans, Jews, and even Orthodox Christians and other Christian 'heretics' were considered 'enemies of God,' outside the pale of frith and fair game for conquest. (I might note that the same attitude was held by leaders of other faiths and tribal beliefs as well. These attitudes have led followers of many religions toward efforts to conquer followers of other religions and their lands, over many centuries.)

The only way for 'outsiders' to save themselves from militant Christianity was to convert to the version of Christianity that held the reins of this power, thus entering their 'frith-garth', and even then, the converts were regarded with suspicion.

After centuries of European crusades and wars, the seeds of a different view of frith began to sprout, in Europe and in the land across the sea. These ideas were influenced not only by European and new American philosophers, but also by contact with Native American tribal customs. These seeds sprouted into the Constitution of the United States, which presented a new view of how frith can be established and maintained on a national level, though the older roots of frith still continue.

This new view presented *ideals and principles* as the core of loyalty around which a folk in frith with one another could gather. Frith-oaths were not sworn to a king or other person, nor to an office such as 'the president', but to the ideals and principles upon which the new nation was founded. This was truly a new thing, a whole new vision and foundation for the establishment and practice of national frith.

Unfortunately, though in principle all people were covered under the Constitution, in practice some people were included in the Constitutional frith-garth, and others were not, leading to struggle, strife, injustice and bitterness throughout the centuries of USA existence and continuing into today. The idea of basing frith upon a social contract, as we do in this country, creates an inspiring ideal for some, and a sense of insecurity for others. In practice, there are different interpretations of what a given culture's or country's social contract is, who is included in it, how it should be maintained and defended, how it should be implemented, how it should be modified or replaced as needed, and who is in charge of all these things.

We can see in the events of the last several years, culminating in the Capitol riot of January 6, 2021, a clash between two different concepts of frith-loyalty. One group held fierce loyalty toward a specific person, Donald Trump. Abstract national ideals and principles were used in service to their leader, his power, and through him to their own power. Their passion of frith was constellated around the personhood of their leader.

The other group's frith-loyalty was to the norms of US constitutional and electoral practice. Any leader they elected was expected promote these norms, and if they did not, they would be argued with and voted out of office. Their leaders were considered replaceable, and were considered as a representative of governing ideals, not as a person in a position of sovereignty. This group's passion of frith was constellated around the ideals themselves.

It is obvious that I am greatly oversimplifying the situation; there were many other complicating and contradictory elements. I am doing so to illustrate my point: much of the strife in our country is based on differing ideas about frith, what frith is based on, who is included in it, and how it is rightfully maintained.

Frith contains within it some basic contradictions that can drive frith-seekers toward conflict as well as toward peace. I think that a deep understanding of these complexities of frith is necessary for any group of people who truly want to maintain frith. It is not a simple process with clear and obvious measures to be taken. Frith, like all human undertakings, has its own pitfalls, and we need to understand them in order to work successfully toward frith at all levels, including our practice of Heathenry.

## Frith-Pitfall 1: Group Dynamics

There are a number of pitfalls as well as many benefits of frith, but I am going to mention only two of them here, that are of sharp relevance to today's circumstances. One is the fact that, whether we like it or not, one of the strongest ways to create frith within a group is to set it against another group, or against outsiders generally. The more strongly people are identified with their own group, and contrast themselves with other groups and outsiders, the stronger the frith is likely to be, *within* that group. It becomes clear to this group that the more 'outsiders' are regarded as 'enemies', the more essential it is to be able to depend on the frith and loyalty of your own group in order to survive. This is a time-honored and popular tactic of politicians around the world, to distract their people from internal problems by focusing on external threats (real or imagined) against their country or group, which fans the flames of group-loyalty. This is also the dynamic that plays in developing stereotypes and prejudices against people who are different from your own in-group.

Some people who have had experience of such tightly-knit 'us versus them' groups find that the strong degree of frith that exists within the group is very attractive and reassuring, and the apparently looser degree of commitment and loyalty outside such groups is lacking in strength and meaning for them. This occurs among religious groups, for example the Amish and other plain folk, who set themselves apart from others in many different details of their lives, in a very peaceful way. They are not hostile toward outsiders, but their ways of maintaining frith and conformity within their group are very strong and sometimes difficult to follow.

Many other religious groups have their own ways of creating an in-culture, such as dietary rules, clothing, religious practices, even language, that distinguish them from others. Most of these are examples of normally harmless ways to create the strong frith of an in-group, without creating much or any hostility toward out-groups: creating 'characteristic and treasured distinctions' as opposed to 'prejudice and hostility.' And of course, there are many non-religious examples of different cultures and languages that can do the same: maintain 'treasured distinctions' within their own group, without directing hostility to those outside their groups.

Unfortunately, *any* distinctions and differences can be used to create hostility and attitudes of superiority / inferiority, if people are determined to do that. In reaction, many well-intentioned modern Westerners feel that distinctions between people should be' denied, ignored, or downplayed in some other way, so as to remove these sources of hostility and social friction. Many people feel very much at home in this more loose and open environment, while others feel that their roots of individual and group identity are erased thereby.

Some people want and value the very strong frith and loyalty that can occur within an in-group, however that group is defined. When the values upon which their in-group is based are threatened, they draw together defensively, reacting with hostility towards outsiders, and with stronger loyalty toward their own. The outsiders then mass against the in-group because of its increased hostility, and escalation ensues. We are all experiencing this collective social misery and anger very widely in today's world, and in my view, the unexamined or unconscious dynamics of frith are a primary driver of this phenomenon.

One example of this which especially comes to mind is the Q-Anon cult, with their powerful motto of in-group frith: "Where we go one, we go all." Interviews with many members, and studies of this phenomenon, point out the importance of group cohesion, of belonging and support, that followers feel they gain from this cult, and which was missing for them before they encountered the cult. Their in-group frith is very strong and rewarding to its members, and is their primary reason for belonging. It is rigidly maintained through hostility of attitude and action toward out-groups. The impenetrability of the frith-barrier (in the form of rigid and baffling beliefs) between this group and the outside world is a great source of frustration and concern for the rest of society. This is a textbook example of the power and dynamics of in-group frith, and of frith's pitfalls.

The need for frith-groups is something that is based in human nature and survival. Our physical survival and social needs are dependent upon our groups: our family and community, our society and economy, and various other imbedded or nested groups that we are a part of. We've evolved to engage in cooperative behavior, but also to draw together in solidarity with those we trust, those who are 'like us', when we, or our values, feel threatened.

I think that our modern efforts to create and extend frith through our society need to take that into account. The larger and more diffuse the group is, the harder it is to maintain the level of personal frith, loyalty, trust, interaction, self-sacrifice, help and support that a tightly knit small group can give: the core of frith itself. When this core of frith is missing, many people seek it in ways that increase unfrith in society as a whole, for example, disadvantaged and rootless youths who join gangs so as to have a place to belong and people they hope will support and defend them.

It's really interesting to see the phenomenon playing out today, of the strong shift between the older form of frith as personal relationships and personal loyalty, into this relatively newer form of frith as adherence to an ideal, to principles, and to people's view of what the social contract is. The result is that frith is spread much more widely than it could be when it depends on face-to-face personal relationships. "People who agree with my ideals and principles" can be found around the world, people whom I will never meet and who may be very different from me in a number of ways, but still a frith-garth develops among us. This is a great feeling, a great and hopeful change in human behavior.

Unfortunately, the pitfalls of frith also grow larger and wider in this environment. Even though the groups within a frith-garth have grown exponentially larger, more encompassing of different people living in different places, the coagulating principle of the group still acts as an in-group trigger.

The expansion of the frith-garth, but in a way that adds to unfrith, can also be seen in the expression of kin-frith. Nowadays, kindreds and clans in our society seldom feud with each other, but groups that perceive their members as being racially related and outsiders as unrelated, unfortunately do so, all around the world. In other words, the issues around racial / ethnic stereotypes and attitudes are an expansion of older kin-frith attitudes, where all one's loyalty belongs to kin, and 'outsiders' don't count. Nowadays, for many people of different races / ethnicities around the world, 'my kin' has been expanded to 'my race / ethnicity', but it still maintains the 'us versus them' in-group frith dynamic. It would seem that expanding the frith-garth to include more people within it should improve frith and tolerance overall, but it doesn't always turn out that way.

Every frith-group coagulates around a set of values that are of great, overriding importance to them. And when they perceive those values to be threatened, they instinctively bunch together and react with hostility, in the time-honored way it's been done for millennia. The opposing group, in turn, feels threatened by the insults and challenges to their own values, and reacts the same way, and again, escalation ensues. In-group frith, again and unfortunately, leads to inter-group hostility.

Then, in an effort to maintain ever-stronger bonds of in-group frith, the group exerts more pressure toward group-think, or at least, pressure to not talk about your ideas if they question any of the values of the group. Eventually this pressure builds, and leads to friction and unfrith within the group, and often to separation or breakup. We've all seen many instances of this happening in our own experiences, I'm sure, including within families, religious groups, political parties, and many other types of groups.

## Frith-Pitfall 2: The Tolerance Dilemma

So, that's one of the pitfalls I wanted to highlight: the natural dynamic of groups which creates in-group frith and inter-group unfrith or active hostility. The other is a very difficult existential dilemma. Tolerance for opposing viewpoints and for behavior, appearance, etc. that is different from oneself is, in principle, a strong promoter of frith. It's something that many modern cultures and societies are trying to move toward, for that reason: it promotes frith, and when frith prevails, many other crucial social benefits follow. So, tolerance in principle is frith-promoting and social-benefit promoting. Tolerance is built into the USA Constitution, as an example of an honored social contract: tolerance of free speech, freedom of conscience (religion), public assembly, etc. These are foundational values for Americans.

But what about tolerance of unfrithful words or behavior, tolerance of intolerance? These things could promote unfrith and disrupt the hoped-for social benefits of frith, and many feel that intolerance should not be tolerated because of the perceived dangers and unfrith arising from it. Our laws attempt to address intolerant behavior that results in violence or criminal actions, and the current unrest in our country is prompting evaluations of these laws and their enforcement, to further improve and, more importantly, implement them fairly and consistently.

But there is a large and difficult gray area, that lies between 'outright criminal action and physical harm' on one end, and 'frithful tolerance of differences' on the other end. Laws and their enforcement deal, or should deal, with one end of this spectrum, while our Constitutional freedoms address the other end. That leaves a large gray area in the middle, that is a subject of much strife and disagreement in our society today. Much of that disagreement involves interpretations of all these matters: how far do personal freedoms extend; what constitutes 'criminal harm' to another person; how should tolerance and rights be enforced when they conflict with each other?

There truly are no easy answers to any of these questions, and those of us who try to think deeply and seriously about these matters often feel we are being thrown into a state of cognitive dissonance or impossible contradictions. For those who highly value tolerance, how far can intolerance be tolerated? How can conflicting personal and constitutional rights be balanced against each other, in a way that promotes the greatest level of frith within society? How can we form frith-groups which highly value tolerance, without triggering the group dynamics I mentioned earlier, which lead groups to bunch up into tighter and tighter group-think when confronted with non-conforming ideas, resulting in an in-group state of idea-intolerance and unfrithfulness? Contradictions and dissonances run rife here, within our frith-garths and within our country and our world as a whole.

## 'Distinctions' versus 'Triggers'

Here are a few very simple thoughts about this, thoughts which many people share and are working hard to implement. How do we approach a frithful understanding of 'differences'? The cohesion of frith-garths, or of any kind and size of groups, fundamentally depends on 'defining who we are', what our basic values and identifiers are, that bring us together as a group. In the process of doing that, it's tempting to think that whatever 'who we are' consists of, it's better in some way than 'who we are not'. This in turn sets up a dynamic that leads to unfrith toward outsiders. Group dynamics can lead to us making the definition of 'who we are' tighter and tighter, and to the ones who get to define 'who we are' becoming a smaller and more authoritarian subset of the group.

All of this arises from devaluing 'who we are not', not wanting to be 'like them', whatever that involves. In order to defend against becoming 'like those others, not-us', the group is willing to compromise in-group frith and out-group frith, and become rigidified. To counteract this dynamic, it's necessary to shift our attitude toward 'differences', and the only way to do that is to do two things: seek a true, respectful, and nonjudgmental understanding of those differences, and allow that to lead us toward not fearing those differences, or fearing them less.

This whole dynamic of 'differences' is rooted in fear: a powerful, primal emotion that can overwhelm all other considerations when it takes over. 'Distrusting those who are different from us,' and distinguishing between 'us' and 'not-us' (whatever cues we use to make this distinction), are instinctive survival strategies, present in animals as well as humans.

Changing such instinctive behavior is truly difficult for all of us; we are working against our instincts and evolutionary behavior, working against certain strong group dynamics, going against peer pressure, going out on a limb, struggling with contradictory values and viewpoints. This is so difficult, involves so much work, and is so threatening to our internal equilibrium, that many don't feel like even dealing with it, and would rather stick with the status quo.

So, if we take the challenge, then we seek to understand the different 'others' and where they are coming from, and we seek to reduce our fear of what they represent. And we hope and encourage those who are different from us to take the same approach toward us. But there is yet another big pitfall here that many of us fall into: we mistake '*understanding* the ways and reasons that others are different from us' to mean 'trying to *erase or deny* differences between us.' The people whose different values and identities are thus being erased or denied by well-meaning frith-ambassadors understandably feel that they themselves are being personally rejected and even threatened.

The message that is being sent (by both / all sides) is often along the lines of: "I 'understand' where you're coming from, and you're forgiven for that, but really once you understand where I'm coming from, you'll see the light and never look back." This is not true, nonjudgmental understanding at all, and neither is it 'respect'. It is an attitude of superiority and an effort to manipulate people, however well-intended it is. It's the 'missionary approach', which missionaries (religious and secular) very sincerely believe in, and we can see the disruptive impacts of that by looking at the long histories of conversion and colonialism around the world.

I think this dynamic explains so many failures of frithweaving. None of us takes well to having our treasured identities, values and beliefs erased or denied, whatever they are. Fear of having this happen drives a great deal of unfrith, strife and friction on all sides of our society, and leads to people and groups taking defensive and hostile positions against each other. 'Differences' thus morph into 'triggers' that set off hostile attitudes and behaviors.

*Differences between people are not going to go away,* whether it's differences of ideas, lifestyles, appearance, physical nature, gender, ability, behavior, beliefs, politics, language, culture, religion, or any other differences. People treasure these distinctions and base their identities on them, among other things. They want to be accepted for them, and fear being denied, rejected or erased because of them. This includes every single person on this planet.

Thus, I believe that the frithful way of approaching differences is to respect and acknowledge their existence and the importance they have for others, even when they seem alien or meaningless to us. Even further, even more big-hearted, is to appreciate and even cherish the distinctions that matter to others, when at all possible, as being something that adds richness, interest, depth and strength to our society, our culture, our life. Cultural distinctions can be cultural treasures, rather than threats, when understanding and appreciation are emphasized and fear is minimized. The celebration of many forms of diversity is something that has grown greatly in the last few decades, providing us all with great enrichment.

Yet some areas of diversity are still excluded from acceptance by many; in fact, they are not recognized as having 'diversity-value', they are regarded as nuisances, crimes, or 'sins'. During the last few decades, 'ideas, values, political positions, beliefs' are among the major differences between people that have been pushed into the area of 'major crimes and sins' that 'the other side is committing against us', rather than being seen by both / all sides as the kind of diversity that can be recognized and accepted as part of a balanced and flexible society, a diverse social ecosystem, that is trying to step back from an overabundance of group-think and 'mono-culture'.

We have, and are working on improving, laws and customs that are supposed to keep 'differences' from sliding into crime and serious harm toward others, whether physical, psychological, financial, reputation, or other types of harm. We need to keep close watch on how those laws and practices are formulated, enforced, respected, and improved as needed. We also have embedded in our social contract the freedoms that allow differences and allow the expression of those differences. Those too need to be respected, especially with regard to those who disagree with us, whose differences are in the form of ideas, thoughts and attitudes.

For all of us in the modern world, where a deep foundation of frith now lies in loyalty to ideas and ideals, this is a very challenging situation. Our struggles are similar to those of the past, where, I'm guessing, there were people who recognized that kin-frith and leader-follower frith often contributed to more strife outside the frith-garth than would have occurred without the rules of these frith-garths, but found it difficult to figure out what to do about it.

I think that the solution that gradually evolved was indeed what we have now: frith based on ideas and ideals, where it is easier to include more people within the 'ideals' frith-garth than it is within kin-garths or oathed war-band garths. But even though this change expands the frith-garth in admirable ways, the dynamics of frith are still operational, its pitfalls and shortcomings as well as its strengths.

## Heathen Frith Today

At its very simplest and most superficial, frith roughly equates to our modern idea of 'peace' in the sense of 'lack of strife.' At its deepest and most powerful, frith is the very fabric of the social bond itself. A community, however small or large, founded upon frith is not a loosely-tied conglomeration of individuals, but one which is truly functional as a coherent body, brought together by a common set of unifying principles, beliefs, customs and practices.

A core understanding about frith is that it is not 'strife-free'. Strife can indeed occur between people who are in frith with each other, though there are limits to the severity of expression allowed. Strife is a natural component of existence: consider its linguistic connection to the word 'strive,' a word that expresses part of the Heathen world-view. Strife only becomes dangerous when there is no frith, no committed relationship with recognized rules and patterns of behavior, to control and counterbalance it.

Heated discussions and arguments about things that matter actually *support* frith, if they are appropriately pursued, because they allow us to share with each other the things that matter most to us. They allow us to be seen as who we really are by our fellow Heathens, and be accepted and respected for who we are, even by those who disagree with us. And we can strive to do the same for others. We keep in mind that our thoughts and opinions are important to each of us, but so is the frith, the social bond we share. *This frith-bond is shallow, unless we share our deeper selves with each other,* the deep thoughts of our Hugr-souls, even in the face of disagreement.

In summary, the woven fabric of frith is the foundation of all human relationships, of cooperative endeavors, and of society as a whole. It is essential for human wellbeing. All systems of ethics, laws, courtesy, diplomacy, customs, proper behavior and the like, are designed to support frith in some form. Frith nevertheless has its pitfalls; it can be both supported, and undermined, by group dynamics.

My purpose in this essay is not to provide any magical solutions (I wish it were that easy!), but to emphasize *the importance of being aware of the powerful dynamics of frith, both positive and negative.* Only by full awareness can we thoughtfully shape our own attitudes, behavior, words and deeds, and thus make a welcoming, respectful, frithful space for others to join us in the creation of true and stable frith-garths that bless this world of Midgard.

## Friendship Verses

*Here is a selection of verses from the Havamal that I adapted*
*to form a poem or song that focuses on frith and friendship.*
*The first / last verse is mine.*

Frith and friendship fail not while faring
Boldly along the byways of Worlds.
'Bare is back without brother behind it':
Frith makes friend the fairest of kin.

Always while young alone I traveled;
Ever and again I wandered from my way.
I knew myself wealthy when I found a friend:
Man is the joy, the joy of man!

Now, an untrusty friend lives too far away,
Even though their path lies right upon your road.
But it's no distance to one who is dear,
Though you fare far over mile after mile.

Always be faithful, always keep troth,
Never be the first to fail in friendship.
Grief grips the heart* that must ever be wary,
Keeping itself always hidden away.
(*Hugr)

## Frith

True bonds are formed when folk keep faith,
Hiding not their hearts from one another.
Anything's better than breach of friendship:
A true friend will say what you'd rather not hear!

No need to give away great gifts always,
Small things are very often enough.
Half a loaf and a lifted horn
Oft and again have found me a friend.

If you have faith in a friend of yours,
Fare you to find them again and again.
Brushwood and grass will soon grow high,
Covering the path no wayfarer walks.

Frith and friendship fail not while faring
Boldly along the byways of Worlds.
'Bare is back without brother behind it':
Frith makes friend the fairest of kin.

A friend offers wise counsel or rede.

# 6. Webs of Luck and Wyrd

## Interplays and Impacts on Events

*Flows of might and main: Hidden paths of Heathen wisdom.*

Luck, wyrd, and the interactions between the two play a vital role in the history, philosophy, metaphysics, and activities of Germanic peoples throughout history. Here I will sort out some of the many strands that seem to me most significant and useful. These can give us an idea of the important and pervasive role luck and its relationship with wyrd played among our elder kin, including the roles of luck and wyrd in forcible conversions from Heathen troth to Christianity.

These ponderings may be useful for modern Heathens in understanding the processes of luck and wyrd in our own lives, both as individuals and as Heathen collectives. I argue that there is a close connection between a belief in luck, and one's ethical choices and actions, and I explore aspects of this connection in my essay here.

Ancient Heathens had more than one word for general 'luck', and many compound words to show the different types and domains of luck. *Sael, saell, saeld* appeared widely in the old Germanic languages, and meant 'luck, good fortune, prosperity, blessing, happiness,' and related concepts. Here are some examples of different kinds of *saell* a person might have:

*Arsaell* = luck with fertility of land, crops, and livestock.
*Byrsaell* = luck with seafaring and sailing weather.
*Kinsaell* = luck in one's kindred: numerous, prosperous, frithful, of good reputation.
*Sigrsaell* = victory luck, battle luck.
*Vinsaell* = luck with friendships and patronage.

*Heill* was another word for luck, and included the concepts of health, wholeness, luck, good fortune, blessing, and so on. In terms of translation into modern languages, there doesn't seem to be much difference between the *heill* and *saell*, though when I look through ancient writings I get the impression of subtle differences. An important type of *heill* one might possess is *Ordheill,* the luck or power of using words to cause either good or harm, as in blessing or cursing. The scholar Vilhelm Grønbech describes *Ordheill* as a "wish charged with power," expressed verbally (p. 147). Another meaning for Ordheill is that people speak well of the person who has it; he or she has the good luck of an excellent reputation. *Mannheill* is the good fortune of getting along well with others (*mann* means 'person' of any gender). *Illa heill* is bad luck.

Old English had the word *sped* (pronounced 'speed'), still used occasionally in old-fashioned phrases such as 'Godspeed' or 'God speed the work / journey, etc.,' meaning good fortune and success in one's endeavor: literally God's luck or blessing on the work. 'Speed' meant luck, success, prosperity, wealth, abundance, opportunity. Its opposite, *wansped* (relating to 'waning') meant poverty, misfortune,

98

failure, lack. Of great importance, as I shall discuss in the next sections, was the King's Speed and the good it could bring to battle, land, fertility, prosperity, opportunities and so forth. The king held an enormous amount of luck within himself, and could spread it around into many domains of action, while according to an old Scandinavian proverb, "poor folk have but one luck, and that a slender one." (Grønbech vol. 1, p. 138.) Other types of 'speed' that one might have include *freondsped* or friend-speed, and *tuddorsped*, which is good fortune with one's offspring: many healthy children blessed with prosperity, good luck, and offspring of their own.

The whole Germanic concept of 'luck' was complex, nuanced, many-faceted, with many words used to express these facets. In fact, Grønbech suggests it makes more sense to use the term 'lucks,' plural, because of the many types and characteristics of luck that were referred to in ancient sources, folklore and folk practices. His view was that these lucks were indeed of different kinds and sources, not all expressions of one single thing. The difference between a king and a thrall was not simply the amount of luck each possessed, but the character of their lucks, as well (p. 171-2).

"Every luck is of its own sort. To go out fishing with a cattle-breeder's particular luck would give the same result as if one tried to catch cod with a ploughshare; to rule and give fertility to the East with a luck that pertained to the West was no less topsy-turvy." (Grønbech p. 168.) Let's explore here some of the important roles of these 'lucks' in the various domains of life.

## The Nature and Role of Luck

Grønbech discusses at length the connection between luck and rede, and I believe this is a very important insight, useful for modern Heathen life as well as ancient. 'Rede' refers to advice, counsel, guidance, but also to one's own rede to oneself: one's experience, learning, thought, intuitions applied to solve problems, meet challenges, and generally conduct one's life successfully. Our ancient kin easily recognized those who were 'rede-y,' guided by wise rede whether from others or within themselves, versus those who were 'unrede-y' and just seemed to get everything wrong no matter how hard they seemed to try. When this unrede-y person was a king, this spelled disaster for his reign.

Rede can be seen as a process, a series of steps leading to action and outcome. By interacting with others (including spiritual beings such as Deities, *Disir, Alfar, fylgjur)* one mingles their rede with one's own thoughts and motivations to form an idea, then a resolution to act in some way, then a plan, and then applies one's own strengths, abilities, resources, and connections to carry out this resolution. This action can be anything: planting a vegetable garden, going into battle or a sports game, frithweaving, planning your home-making or work tasks for the week, traveling, studying, whatever. The outcome of these actions shows what kind of luck one has, and the lucks of any who are associated with the process.

It is not only the outcome, it is the entire process that involves and displays one's lucks or unluck. All of the steps in the process, says Grønbech, are nothing other than luck

100

applied to one's own or to others' affairs (p. 144). One's luck is intimately associated with one's rede, both internal and external sources of rede. This insight leads directly to the role of spirit beings in our luck or unluck, a topic I discuss in following sections.

"Luck stretches in one continuity from the core of man's mind to the horizon of his social existence, and this, too, is indicated in the meaning of rede, which comprises the state or position of a man, his influence and competence. The inner state of a man in luck is described in Icelandic as a whole mind, *heill hugr.* ...The man of whole mind is true to his kin and his friends, stern to his enemies, and easy to get on with, when lesser men come seeking his aid. His redes are really good gifts to the receiver – whole redes, in Icelandic *heill rað.*" (Grønbech p. 148-9.)

"The ancient word rede...is a perfect illustration of Teutonic psychology. When given to others, it means counsel; when applied to the luck working within the mind, it means wisdom, or a good plan, and from an ethical point of view, just and honest thoughts. But the word naturally includes the idea of success, which accompanies wise and upright devising, and on the other hand power and authority, which are the working of a sound will." (Grønbech p. 148)

A good example of the importance of wise rede can be seen when comparing a king possessing war-speed, versus a traditional berserker as we read of in the sagas. The berserker might be equally victorious in his battles, but he lacks rede, forethought, ethical motives and behavior. His comrades and leader might find his victory luck useful, but this is

101

counterbalanced by the degree of unluck and destructiveness he brings to all parts of life not relating to battle.

Here we see that luck, rede, and right thought and action interact and lead into and out of each other. Luck enables one to keep frith, honor, friendship, promises and oaths, to carry out plans successfully, and to refrain from acting dishonorably. It's interesting to note that the words most often used to translate 'good' and 'evil' in the Gothic-language Bible are respectively *sels* and *unsels*, the same words listed above *(saell)* to mean luck and unluck. All of these points show a connection between luck and ethical action.

## Downsides of Luck

By the same token, unluck can both lead to, and result from, unethical and unwise action. Grønbech points out that great unluck results from killing a woman, a dishonorable act, and that "unluck will sooner or later arise in a place where dishonor has manifested" (Grønbech p. 155). Luck and unluck are considered contagious, able to spread from person to person, and between persons and places or objects. The luck of healing is one form of contagion, where the healer's healing-luck is spread through his or her luck-power to the person, animal or place that needs healing.

Another form of luck-contagion is the power a king has of passing his luck on to his followers: directly by his presence, word or touch, or indirectly through his gifts of objects such as weapons or ornaments which carry his luck, and even through word of mouth messages sent to the recipient of his luck. The unluck of a dishonorable act such as oath-breaking can spread to friends and associates of the actor, especially if they had supported him or her in some way or were oath-bound to the actor.

Luck seems like a very positive phenomenon! But it definitely had its downsides in the thought and experiences of our elder kin. Relationships among people involve power in various forms, and they regarded luck as the essence of this power to win, to succeed, thrive, and even to survive. All depended on the type and amount of luck one had, as well as that of one's kin, associates, patrons and allies.

In deciding whether to risk a confrontation or challenge toward another person or group, it was essential to examine the degree of luck your side could bring to bear, and the luck of the other side. "You have not luck to measure yourself against a king," Kveldulf says to his angry son Thorulf, as Grønbech quotes (p.157), and goes on to say that "every trial of strength between men was a strife between two powers of luck, a spiritual conflict."

When two lucks clashed with one another, or a powerful luck attacked a weaker one, dire consequences resulted for the weaker party. "If a plan really has life in it, then it can only be checked by a greater luck killing it. ...It (the greater luck) can lay itself like a nightmare upon a poorer man's luck and make it barren and confused" (Grønbech p. 144).

"The luck of every yeoman, every chieftain, was a character, with its peculiarities, its strengths and weaknesses, its eccentricities, and linked throughout to a certain property

(Grønbech p. 171)." The 'property' to which luck is linked could be a kingdom, a farm, a region, even a hut, as well as weapons and other objects; this will be further discussed, below. The peculiarities and characteristics of one's luck or unluck shaped one's life and deeds. Many – perhaps all – of the tragic deeds and circumstances that we read about in the sagas and poems can be considered the result of the hero's luck or unluck: all the confusion with Siegfried / Sigurd and Brunnhilde / Sigrdrifa, Gudrun, and others that we read about in the tale of the *Nibelungs / Volsungs* are at root the workings of luck in their lives, showing the power and inescapability of luck and unluck. Grønbech quotes the *Volsungasaga:* "Sinfjotli is taunted with his violent career in these words: 'All unluck came upon you, you killed your brothers'" (p. 152).

An understanding of the Germanic king's luck gives a good deal of insight into the nature of luck itself. As Grønbech notes, Germanic kings had very little formal power, in terms of a constitution, laws, statutes, any kind of structural authority. A king held his position by virtue of his superior luck, and if he was 'rede-less' he was in a very poor position to exert any authority or rule (pp.161-3). The idea of 'divine right' of kings had not yet developed; on the other hand, the king's speed or luck was a clear indicator of the Gods' blessing on both king and folk.

If we stop to think about it, there is a big difference between the ideas of 'divine right' versus 'the Gods' blessing as shown by luck, speed and rede.' Divine right is claimed, rather than proven, and rests only upon authoritative statements by church and royalty themselves. A king's luck (and the luck of any leader), on the other hand, is continually proven by his rede and deeds, and if it fails, his folk have reason enough to disregard, disrespect, distrust, or even displace him.

## The Roots of Luck and Unluck

So, where does all this luck and speed come from? How do people gain it or lose it? There are a number of sources for luck, and causes for its loss. One root that was very important to our elder kin was the *hamingja*, the luck and spiritual power, that could reside in objects and in land. This phenomenon is an example of the 'contagiousness' of luck. An heirloom, a weapon, jewelry and ornaments, even household and farm implements – anything used by humans, really, would pick up luck or unluck from its users. The longer the item was used in a rede-full, successful, appropriate way, the more luck it accumulated. Thus, heirlooms passed down in the family line were very powerful donors of luck to each of their owners and their kin.

Hamingja-filled or luck-filled objects (including parcels of land), used as gifts and pledges, were of fundamental importance to significant alliances of any kind: marriage, political alliance and patronage, frithweaving, partnerships and business contracts. It was important to speak or 'lay' the luck honestly into the gift by stating that the luck or value is being given with the object at the time of giving. This is an expression of the virtue of generosity: giving the complete gift, with its luck, with a true heart.

Often people tried to 'cheat' by giving an object, but either failing to give the luck / hamingja with it, or by ill-speaking or ill-wishing the exchange, thus nullifying the luck or changing it to bad luck. The same principles applied if the object was being purchased or bartered: any luck inherent in the object was an important part of its value, and needed to be handled appropriately.

The hamingja and luck of an object, a piece of land, even a domestic animal, was damaged or destroyed by the following deeds: betrayal, breaking one's word or bargain, by unworthy use or misuse of it, and even by unauthorized use. For example, unauthorized 'borrowing' of a bull to service one's cow, and then returning the bull, would damage the bull's potency, its ability to sire hamingja-filled offspring. The quality of its seed would decline, and thus decrease the luck of its owner. The luck given by the potent bull depends on the proper relationship between owner and bull, and when this relationship is damaged by unauthorized use – an expression of disrespect and dishonor – luck is lost all around. (Grønbech p. 78)

Looking at ancient tales and poetry, it is easy to see how valuables gained by theft, especially multiple theft such as stealing a dragon's hoard which was itself stolen by the dragon, brought great unluck with them, such as told in the *Nibelungenlied* with its cursed treasure hoard acting balefully down the generations. The same did not, apparently, always apply to battle loot, especially if the loot was then given to the victorious warriors with words of praise by their leader in a luck-filled symbel.

Another source of unluck was power-filled words used against a person. "Words could bite through luck and fix themselves in a man. ...They had life in them, they would creep about inside the victim, hollowing him out until there was no strength left in him, or they would change him and mould him according to their own nature." (Grønbech p.146.) This was an important reason for the boasting and threats exchanged with the enemy right before a battle began: each trying to weaken the others' battle-speed through the power carried in words. This is also how curses and spells would work, by damaging the victim's luck, whether it was health-luck, love-luck, wealth-luck, or whatever. These are expressions of *ordheill*, word-luck, which also could be used for blessing and good luck.

Luck was also gained, as discussed earlier, by association with people of good rede and strong luck, especially kings or chieftains. These leaders obtained and held their positions through their rede, luck and speed, giving full proof that they had luck in abundance. The leaders gained loyal followers through the exercise of their rede (good counsel, wise plans) and luck / speed (successful deeds), and the followers gained luck themselves by association. Luck could be passed on through gifts, words, touch, and even strong intent alone.

Any frithful relationship offered the opportunity for people to share in one another's luck, as long as they maintained the relationship through right and rede-full thoughts, words and behavior. "With the flourishing of frith go luck and well-being" (Grønbech p. 149). What is perhaps

different about their thinking compared to ours, though, is
that frith and other fortunate states of being were more often
considered the result of luck, rather than luck being the result
of frith. In other words, if you have the right kind of luck
(frith-speed, *mannheill)*, then frithful relations come easily
to you; if you have unluck in this area, then frith is difficult
to maintain. Then, breaking or damage of frith adds more to
the unluck you already have.

Luck or unluck, very importantly, came from one's
kindred, from the bloodline. Kin-luck depends on past deeds
of the family, their honor, and the luck of each kinsman. It
also depends on the hamingja stored within their family
heirlooms, possessions, and land. As we know, Germanic folk
laid great emphasis on the ability of the past to shape the
present. For each person, the past is solidified through the
family line; each person in the present inherits the influence,
for good or ill, of the past through their kin.

This might play less of a role for many people in
modern life, but its influences are not absent: our genes, our
attitudes, our culture, are inherited from our kin nowadays
just as they were in the past. It's worthwhile to examine our
inheritance of rede / luck / unluck, see how to make the most
of rede and luck, and limit the unluck, that we each inherit
from our kin.

Kings and chieftains sent their hamingja / luck into
their land through their rule and their connection with their
folk. Ordinary farmers and land-holders would bring their
own land under their luck by working and using it rede-fully,
using tools full of hamingja as a way of inserting their luck

into the land. Land-holders were themselves under the rule of chieftains, who would hold the larger regions under their luck.

"The luck of the local chieftain was absolute, but could only answer to the soul of the valley, the district, and the people…it might extend to the fishing grounds…or seafaring expeditions undertaken by the villagers; but in order to cover other lands and other communities it had first to undergo a transformation by drawing up the alien power (the unique luck of that area of land) into itself and assimilating it. …To defend or conquer Norway called for the luck of a Harald." (Grønbech p.168.)

Fertility, good seasons, and frith were the outcome of the luck of landholders, great and small, and in turn the luck of the land supported those who used and lived on it.

As far as I understand, luck does not get used up or wear out. As I've described above, though, it can be outclassed and overcome by someone with greater luck, or lost by being associated with a deed of great unluck. If one's luck is attached to, or comes through, a spirit being, it can be withheld by the spirit, or the spirit may leave, temporarily or permanently, if it is displeased or disrespected. It is also possible to follow a path that is lucky at the beginning, but following it too far ends up 'pushing your luck,' shifting it into its opposite of unluck. Too many gamblers have discovered this, to their loss.

## Givers and Mediators of Luck

All of the sources of luck I described above were important, but, especially for an ordinary individual, the most important source of luck was the presence, nature, and actions of various spirit beings. These beings are familiar to modern Heathens: the Norns, greater and lesser; the *fylgja* (an accompanying spirit in animal or human form) and *kinfylgja* (the fylgja who follows the kin-line), the *hamingja-spirit*, *disir* and *alfar* (powerful ancestral spirits), landwights, *tomte, heinzelmann, kabauter*, and many other spirits of home and farmland, and of course the Gods and Goddesses, some more associated with luck than others.

Other nature spirits, such as water-wights, wood-elves and so forth, might play a role if one encountered them personally – often a negative role if a wild wight was angered by trespass, for instance, and cursed the trespasser. True disaster could come upon a farmer, his land, crops, cattle and kin, if he angered a powerful wight. On the other hand, centuries of folk practice tell us that the elves and other wights can be benevolent as well, when given offerings and treated well. All of the gifts and curses of these beings consist of luck in various forms, for example gaining or losing fertility of farm and family, word-luck in the form of good rede or the gift of poetry gained from a mound-wight, or hunting luck.

The involvement of these various spirit beings in our life and luck begins even before conception, as our kin-luck shapes the space we will be born into. Conception, gestation and ensouling are ruled over by powerful beings shaping the

110

implantation of various forms of luck within us, including greater and lesser Norns, kinfylgja, Disir and Alfar, hamingja, and fylgja. The caul and the placenta (afterbirth) are themselves power-filled physical vehicles for luck-bearing spirits, the hamingja and personal fylgja, and if one bears an animal hama / spirit-shape this may gestate along with the fetus as well. Indeed, it is my thought that without the actions of these luck-bearing beings, conception and gestation could not successfully take place at all. I would say that in ancient Heathen thought and traditional folklore alike, luck, for good or ill, is the etheric medium within which all of these processes take place.

As the scholar Jan DeVries describes, the hamingja is the indwelling luck, in the form of a protective spirit that accompanies a person life-long. It also takes the form of a power or energy that can radiate out of a person. The hamr, afterbirth and caul (*Glückshaube* or luck-cowl) contain the soul or a soul-like being, that accompanies a person as a protective spirit. These beliefs are widespread, and certainly go back to Proto-Germanic times, before the Germanic peoples split off from each other, if not even earlier times. The fylgja also follows a person and gives rede and luck. The House-father *(Hausvater)* or founding spirit of the family, the *Tomte* (house and farm spirit), the *Cofgodas* (Anglo-Saxon spirits of the home), *Armaðr* (field and harvest spirit), and others I've listed above, all have in their gift the blessings of luck, and failing to honor them or insulting them will lead to ill luck. (deVries pp. 222ff.)

## A word about the Fylgja

There is a great deal of confusion of terms about accompanying spirits in all the lore, folklore, and scholarly references, that I am not going to sort out here in any detail! There are a few ways to simplify or at least de-confuse this. A useful one is to take the approach that the scholars deVries and Grimm do: they suggest that 'Fylgja' meaning 'follower' is really an umbrella term that covers any kind of accompanying spirit: luck-spirits, ancestral spirits, animal-form spirits, spirits attached to land or home, etc. (See DeVries p. 224ff and Grimm p. 874ff.) This is something like what we do when using the generic term 'landwights' to refer to Nature spirit-beings who come in many different forms and 'species'.

Many modern Heathens translate Fylgja as the 'Fetch', a phenomenon told of in lore of Celtic lands and peoples, where Fetch is understood to be a personal soul who can sometimes externalize itself from a person's body, especially just before and after death. In my understanding of Germanic soul lore, the role described by the idea of the Fetch is actually a function of our Hugr soul.

If you are even more confused about all these terms than before, you're in good company! But let me propose this simplification, which I use when discussing soul lore:

'Fylgja' ('follower') can be used as a generic term that covers all types of spirits who accompany humans and are not part of our own personal, inborn, human 'soular system.'

'Souls' are entities who are members of our own personal 'soular system' and together create our holistic Self.

Some of these souls, in particular the Hugr and Ghost, can exit our body and act independently, both while we are living and after we are dead. Hugr can also take alternate shapes like animals or flying witches when externalized as a 'Hugham', a Hugr with a shape. Thus they can appear as independent spirits, but they are still rooted within us while we are living, part of our 'soular system'.

Ancestral spirits like the Disir (female) and Alfar (male), in my understanding, are the Hugr-souls of departed humans. Thus, a Hugr can be taken for a Fylgja or a Fetch, when encountered outside the body of a living person, or when it is the Hugr-spirit of a dead person.

### Deities and Luck

The connection between our Deities and human luck is, I think, quite a variable and individual matter. Certainly blessings flow from them to us, which express themselves as luck, but my own feeling is that this is a somewhat different dynamic than the kinds of luck I've been discussing here. Sometimes, particularly with complex Deities like Odin, and others too, some of their effects on our lives and on the lives of Heathens in the past can seem more like unluck when viewed and experienced in a superficial manner!

I think this is a deep matter, which is a good subject for prayer and meditation in order to understand the connection between the lucks and unlucks of your life, and the Gods and Goddesses who are closest to you personally. Often what seem like unlucky events and circumstances in our lives are blessings in disguise, as our *fulltrui* (male) and *fulltrua* (female) Deities guide us, teach us, challenge us, and help us develop our full and deep potential as humans and as friends and companions of the Gods. (*Fulltruar* are the specific Deities whom we trust most fully, our closest God-friends.)

I will mention one God here, though, who is very clearly connected with good lucks in the elder lore: Frey. He is the patron of frith, of frithful rule and benevolent kingship, of *Ar* meaning 'harvest', of fruitfulness and good seasons, of fertility and plenty, of mild weather, sun and rain in their seasons, of male potency and fertility, and of good luck generally. He is also closely associated with departed ancestors, another great source of our luck (or in the case of unfortunate ancestors, unluck.)

Other Deities were and are prayed to for specific kinds of luck, as well: for example Ullr or Skadhi for hunting-luck, Frigg and Freya for luck in conception and childbirth, Forseti or Tyr for luck with legal issues or conflicts, Njord for safe and profitable seafaring ventures, and so forth.

The whole issue of luck and unluck in our lives, the big picture, is a very worthy subject for discussion with our closest Holy Ones. Our luck is much influenced by our relationships with them, and by our willingness to attune ourselves to their wisdom and rede.

## Luck and Wyrd

One of the roadblocks to a clear understanding of the ancient viewpoints about the connection between luck and wyrd is the way modern pagans, and our culture generally, have been influenced by Westernized ideas about the Eastern concept of karma. The way karma is understood in our present time and place seems like a very logical and fair way for the universe to work: good deeds are rewarded by good circumstances, most likely in future lives but perhaps in this one, while evil deeds reap ill circumstances. Our present lives and luck are the fruit of our past deeds, good and ill, and we lay the layers of karma for our next lives and luck as we live this one. This seems to fit very well with the ancient Heathen concepts of wyrd and orlay, where the layers of the past give rise to events and circumstances of the present.

The only problem is that I find only the vaguest hints, in the elder lore, that our forebears actually thought this way. There is much more material that indicates a more fatalistic viewpoint: that the Norns hand out our luck, orlay, fate almost randomly when we are born, and that is what we are given to live out our lives. There may be a sudden change, from luck to unluck, at some point in our lives, and this turning point might be connected to an ill deed that brings ill luck. But in ancient thought, this ill deed, this apparently free will action that we think might have been avoided, would have been programmed into our lives from the beginning. Perhaps not the specifics of the deed or event, but the impulse within ourselves to commit such a deed or to become entangled in ill-luck circumstances, would have been there from the beginning, biding its time.

This is a viewpoint that was common in the ancient world of Greece and Rome, as well, and likely in other ancient cultures. It led to the powerful tragic dramas of the ancient Greek poets, where the hero could not foresee nor avoid the dread workings of fate, and his 'heroism' rested upon the way he responded to his unavoidable fate. The same kind of story-line shows very clearly in the tale of Sigurd / Siegfried and all the others involved in the *Volsungasaga / Nibelungenlied.*

Grønbech discusses "a deep-rooted peculiarity in the psychology of the ancient character. The idea that if one but earnestly wills, then the power (luck in action) will come or that the power may perhaps be there, but the will be lacking, had no validity to the Northman. All his peculiarities were due to the nature of his luck; obstinacy as well as courage, pride....violence....intractability, fearlessness. Luck is the nature of the mind, the character and will. With our ideas as to the reciprocal effects of desire and will, we must again and again in these old sagas find ourselves face to face with insoluble riddles. It often seems as if men would gladly relinquish destructive undertakings, ...gladly clear away misunderstandings and enmity, but something invisible leads their endeavors to miss the mark." (p. 158.)

The scholar Jan deVries has a similar take on this subject. The ancient Heathens would not assume that the details of their entire lives were controlled by fate set by the Gods, he writes. Rather, from the beginning to the end of life, there is an inner 'law' which determines its course, that lies in the inner being of the person. Here we can think of the hamingja luck-being, and the fylgja, whose guidance leads to an inner consistency or logical course of life. But, outside of this realm, catastrophes and disasters can occur, breaking into this pattern of normal life, that were attributed to outside forces, to the powers of fate. In many of the tales of war and battle, it is Odin who plays this role as the dealer of fate. (DeVries p. 268)

It's important for us to remember that there was a real difference between 'wyrd' as anciently used, versus 'luck', as these concepts apply to any specific person. *Wyrd* as used in the ancient poetry and tales almost always referred specifically to the time and circumstances of an individual's death. At birth, the circumstances of death were laid by the powers of fate, but the circumstances of the life lived between these two points of birth and death was the domain of luck, and generally not as heavily influenced by the great powers. Rather, it was the smaller powers, the spirit beings such as the *kinfylgja, disir* and *alfar, hamingja*, and so forth, that guided the actions of luck and unluck in their lives.

We must keep in mind, though, that some of these smaller powers of luck had a connection with the Norns and other godly powers. Our personal hamingja-spirit may be assigned to its duty by the Norns, or come into being at the time of the Norn's actions as they lay orlay and shape our Aldr. So, wyrd, in the ancient understanding of an individual's death, was assigned to a person at birth; it was 100% certain and came upon them in the time and way established by the Norns at the beginning of their lives.

Luck is different: it is complex, variable; the outcome of the luck or unluck is not 100% certain in any given circumstance. There are many influences upon each person's luck or unluck, including the lucks of other people with

117

whom one interacts which can have a strong impact on one's own luck.

The meaning of *wyrd* that I discuss, above, refers to an individual's wyrd. Our ancestors also recognized a greater sense of wyrd as an ongoing, ever-flowing cosmic influence, shaping time and events, governed primarily by the Norns and especially Wyrd / Urdh herself. Bauschatz defines the ancient understanding of wyrd as "the influence and control of the past over the present" (p. 88).

Yet, importantly, an ancient Heathen would not try to control the flow of wyrd on his or her own behalf; the notion of being able to do this would not come until long after Christianization. Instead, a person speaking in symbel would try to control their own path, placing themself within the existing flow of wyrd by boasts and oaths and the deeds connected to them. (Bauschatz p. 83.)

This is an important distinction: a Heathen did not attempt to control the flow of wyrd, but rather to control their own deeds and behavior in order to work with, rather than against, the cosmic flow of wyrd.

This is a very significant point in understanding the difference between wyrd and luck. An ancient Heathen would definitely strive to gather all the luck that they could: by associating with those who have greater luck; by obtaining lucky objects, land, etc.; by participating in fortunate enterprises; by listening to the rede of humans or spirits to guide them into the path of luck; by cultivating and propitiating spirit beings who could give luck or unluck. Though it was recognized that luck was given to each person—greater or lesser degrees and types of luck—yet there was always the effort to increase luck and avoid unluck.

There was, however, no thought of being able to change one's wyrd; only, as Bauschatz discusses throughout his book, the effort to place one's deeds within the flow of wyrd and thus give one's deeds and one's name a place in history, and in the woven fabric of space-time itself in the form of the Well and the Tree.

## Wyrd, Luck and 'Karma'

In ancient thought, did wyrd act like karma in the sense that good deeds in one life will lead to good luck or fortunate circumstances in the next life, and evil deeds will lead to misfortune? In other words, is there an ethical connection between 'deeds' and 'wyrd' that attaches to one or more of our souls and carries over? I've seen very little evidence of such a thing, neither in the primary sources of poems and sagas, nor in the analysis and interpretations of modern scholars. The reason a person wanted to place his deeds into the flow of wyrd was for his fame, his name, his reputation, and the rewards that came with that during and after life, as those deeds and fame were associated with himself or herself, by name. Great deeds placed in the flow of wyrd would lead to a famous name, respect, luck, perhaps wealth and success, luck and a good name for one's kindred line and posterity, and hopefully an afterlife in Valhalla or elsewhere that would continue this trend.

There was a belief in reincarnation, at least in certain circumstances, and there was even more evidence of a belief that it was possible to pass luck from one generation to the next. *(Our Troth,* 2nd edition, p. 509.) What was important to them concerning luck and the afterlife was continuing the kin-luck. In the same way that a king or chieftain could pass luck to a follower, a dying person could pass their luck on to a child, not yet born, within the kindred. The dying person would state that they would pass their luck on to a kin-child who would bear their name, an example of the principle that it was most effective to state in words the gift of luck given, to ensure that the transfer of luck was successful. The vehicle, the medium, for the transfer of luck was the name.

In the instances of this transfer of luck upon death that we see in the lore, there is little hint of any belief that this process is related to ethical actions during the person's lifetime, except to the extent that they have maintained their luck well enough for it to be worth passing on. There is not a sense that this passing on of luck is automatic, as it would be with karma: a conscious effort or intention involving giving and naming needs to be made for the transfer to happen.

An interesting thing to note in this context is that even though the person is dying, he or she still has luck to pass on to the next generation. There is no sense, in general, that the person is dying because his or her luck 'ran out,' though there are sometimes references to unluck happening in battle or other circumstances. The dying person has "met their wyrd", "wyrd is very near," "wyrd has come upon them": these are the phrases so often used to describe death in the ancient poetry. A person may be stupendously lucky;

this has no bearing on the fact that one day their wyrd will bring death at a time already determined.

## Luck, Wyrd, and Olaf Tryggvason

It often seems that the connection between wyrd and luck in our ancestors' thoughts becomes more baffling, the more one looks into it! I think I can reasonably say that a modern person expects there to be some connection between personal choice, ethical action (whatever that means within a given culture and time), luck, and wyrd; some sense of 'karma' in action. We have seen instances, particularly from Grønbech, where ethical actions such as honor and frith interact positively with luck. But there are also many instances where luck, such as the luck of King Olaf Tryggvason who was considered mightily lucky, was used to promote violence, unrestrained conquest, cruel and forcible conversion to Christianity, scorn toward the old laws, faith, folkways. His luck was not lessened in the least by being so (mis)used! (See the "History of Olaf Tryggvason" chapter in the *Heimskringla*.) The fact that Olaf continued lucky and successful in these efforts was a main reason why his followers assumed this was the right thing for him to do, and it supported the argument for conversion to Christianity: Christianity as enacted by Olaf brought luck with it, in their minds.

From the perspective of understanding luck and wyrd, what happened here? First Olaf wanted more power and had the luck to get it; then he embraced Christianity as a further source of power and luck; then he rampaged across Norway, brutally forcing conversion on everyone, beating down the lucks of lesser people and communities. He kept gaining luck by his successful endeavors and by putting more and more land and people 'under his luck' as well as under the 'luck of Christianity'. (I might point out here that though Olaf had a lot of victory-luck, he definitely lacked wife-luck, showing Grønbech's point that luck often shows up only in limited areas of life, not overall.)

Once Olaf had stamped down Norway, many people concluded that "Obviously all this was the right thing to do, because Olaf wielded and increased his luck and success, and that is the proof of its rightness!" For them, luck 'justified' Olaf's actions; luck drove the actions while 'ethics' toddled along behind, only catching up at the end rather than being the initial motivation for the actions.

It's difficult to see any ethical lessons in any modern sense in Olaf's tale, any connection between right behavior, luck and wyrd. He worked hard and brutally to destroy Heathen custom, the old laws, practices, and troth with the Holy Ones, which Heathens vigorously objected to and were tortured and killed for their pains. Although the Christians of the time apparently approved his actions and cheered him on, this was entirely a self-interested reaction. Certainly Olaf did not follow Jesus' actual teachings of right behavior, as outlined in the Commandments, the Beatitudes and so forth! It is very doubtful whether Olaf and his advisors knew very much at all about Christianity and Christian ethics; they just followed 'Christianity' as a route to power. So what I am saying is that there was no ethical framework underlying

Olaf's luck: neither Heathen nor Christian ethics were applied, except to the extent that many Heathens and newly converted Christians apparently thought that luck was its own justification.

Thus, luck was considered to play a very prominent role, even the defining role, in this and other conquests. Where is wyrd in this kind of situation? Was it wyrded for Norway to become Christian under the brutal boot of Olaf? Or were Olaf and his followers somehow 'exempt' from wyrd? Were they able to 'conquer' Heathen wyrd and replace it with a Christian one? I think that Christians saw the latter as being the case: Olaf's luck (and the luck of other Christian conquerors in Heathen and Pagan lands) was so powerful that he was able to actually shift wyrd and change it into a new path, using 'Christ's luck' to do so. This was apparently the main reason why many Heathens were willing to convert: 'Christ's luck' was proven by the outcome of the conquest, while Heathen luck was overcome.

## Luck and the Ordeal

These are painful and difficult questions and issues for modern Heathens, especially those of us who like to ponder abstract matters of Heathen philosophy. In situations as I've just described, some very profound questions about the connection between luck and wyrd leap out to grapple with the Heathen inquirer. ("Here be dragons!")

One of the basic issues for us here is the ancient belief that luck – the outcome of an event – demonstrates wyrd. This is the basis for the concept of the Ordeal (an ordeal in the form of a contest between two or more people): whoever wins the ordeal proves that they are 'right' in the sense of being within the flow of both luck and wyrd. The loser in the ordeal has gone against the flow of wyrd, and has no luck in the matter pertaining to the ordeal. An ordeal stands outside the realm of law and ethics; the sole determinant of luck, wyrd, and 'right and wrong' in the situation is: who wins, and who loses?

If we follow the philosophical principle of the ordeal to its logical end, then we have the social situation that pertained in Heathen lands before, during, and after the forcible conversion to Christianity. There were many factors leading to the frequent conflicts, both greater and lesser, that occurred then, including environmental pressures, overpopulation (population greater than the land's carrying capacity), migrations and cultural clashes.

But a major motivation for people was testing and trying their luck, especially important in situations of uncertainty. "Can our army or warband beat theirs? Can I prevail over my neighbor? Can I survive this Viking expedition and make myself rich? Can I win this game of chance, or will I lose everything? Whose luck is stronger, mine or his?" And so on. Life and its activities were seen as ordeals, and the reward, the 'win', was to prove to yourself and to others that both luck and wyrd are on your side.

## Belief in Luck Led to Forcible Conversion

Keeping these points in mind, let's return to the profound question of the meaning of Tryggvason's forcible conversion of Norway to Christianity, and other similar events such as Charlemagne and his Frankish Christians conquering the Heathen Saxons. Was this wyrded? This would be a bitter conclusion for modern Heathens to draw.

Was it not-wyrded, meaning that something stronger than wyrd was at play here? This is also a bitter conclusion for us: ancient Heathen thought was that there is nothing, not even our Gods, that is stronger than Wyrd.

Or thirdly, did Olaf (or the powers of luck behind him) manage to achieve an unprecedented shift from one whole path of wyrd (Heathen) into another one (Christian), the kind of jump or tipping point we see in graphs of modern chaos theory? Bitter, again!

Where does this leave us, if we want to keep troth with Heathen ways and beliefs, but not do so with blind faith alone? The dilemma these questions leave us in looks a lot like an ordeal itself, a challenging test set for us by a dark and challenging deity like Odin or the Norns themselves!

One response to these questions that some modern Heathens believe is that the conversion era corresponded to the death of Baldur and the coming of Ragnarök, and that the modern resurgence of Heathenism shows the beginning of a new cycle of wyrd. This seems to me both a logical and a very meaningful conclusion to draw. In the course of writing this essay, though, and struggling with the question of how luck and wyrd relate to one another, I have some further thoughts along these lines.

The way our ancestors believed in and trusted in luck was at root the cause of their conversion to Christianity.

Christianity was proven, in their minds, to be more powerful than the traditional ways, and therefore more filled with luck. Since they wanted to put themselves in the flow of luck, it made sense for them to convert once this 'luck' was proven. Once the conversion happened, was laid in the Well of Wyrd by its manifestation in history, that showed to their minds what direction the flow of wyrd was taking: this conversion was inevitable. And of course the Christian powers-that-be were glad to take advantage of this conclusion!

## Luck, Ethics, and Troth with the Gods

Now, I suggest that there is another way to look at what was happening, in addition to the Ragnarök theory. I think that the belief and trust in luck had gotten out of hand in the Heathen culture of that time; that it took over all other ethical bases for belief, trust, and behavior, as the most powerful foundation for action and judgment in the world. We can understand how this happened: luck seemed to them to be a good messenger to tell them about the Gods' will, judgment, guidance, as well as a signal indicating the flow of wyrd. These are mysterious forces; it's difficult to figure them out, and very helpful to humans to be given clues in the form of luck and unluck.

I don't deny the value of this, by any means, neither in the past nor in the present. The flow of luck and hamingja is essential to our lives and endeavors in many ways, as I discussed earlier in this essay. But it seems to me that it needs to be balanced with some other very important factors as well.

One of them is a code of ethics, that guides us through flows and events of luck and unluck so that we can keep our eyes on a higher, longer-term, broader view as well as the everyday ebb and flow of personal events. A code of ethics can be symbolized by the Tyr-Star, the North or Pole star, that guides us and "keeps troth well with Athelings over the mists of night," as the Tiwaz rune-poem tells us.

A Heathen code of ethics (as has been much discussed among Heathens!) is not an authoritative list of commandments handed down from on high. It is something that evolves among Heathens based on what works well for us all, tested by time and circumstance, and it continues to evolve as circumstances change. It is attuned to our Gods and Goddesses, our troth and frith, our customs and traditions. It helps us function well in the modern world while keeping our honor bright and our frith and troth whole and strong.

Along with ethics, our trust in luck needs to be balanced with strong, ongoing interactions with our Deities and with lesser spirits as well. This is an important point to consider: *sometimes apparent 'unluck' is simply a challenge, a lesson, or guidance from our patron Deities or guiding spirits,* and this needs to be interpreted differently than simply assuming we've been cursed with bad luck and everyone is against us! It may be that dealing with our 'unluck' in a manner consistent with today's Heathen ethics will in fact lead us onto a lucky path. In this way, unlucky circumstances in our life can be approached as an *ordeal:* by responding to the ordeal with honorable and ethical choices, we may turn the unluck into luck.

*Sometimes sacrifice is called for, rather than following an apparently lucky path.* We may be asked to give something up in a way that looks unlucky for us, even to the extent of our safety or our life. This is how heroes are made. The unluck happening in our life may be a call from the Holy Ones that something in our life needs to be sacrificed, for their sake, our sake, the sake of others.

When we encounter unluck, this is an important question we need to ask in examining the situation: are we being asked to regard this unlucky situation as a sacrifice? Spend time in prayer, meditation and divination to pursue a clear answer to this question, and to find a path for your response.

Sometimes apparent luck can lead us astray, blinding and deafening us to cues that this course can only lead us so far, that there is a time to stop or change course before the luck shifts to unluck because we've pushed it too far. This dynamic is the basis for most of the tragic dramas and sagas across many different cultures! It's also the reason countless people around the world and across the centuries have lost all their wealth and wellbeing, by blindly pursuing good luck past its turning-point into bad luck, and missing or deliberately ignoring all the cues that this was happening.

If 'luck' is the only signal, the only cue that we are attuned to as a way of directing our behavior, it can become a stumbling block in the path of honor, frith, generosity, and all the other Heathen thews or ethics. The pursuit of luck can sometimes lead us into behaving very selfishly when perhaps other values like honor, frith, and troth with the Holy Ones would counsel us quite differently.

## Luck, Rede and Wisdom

Here is where we come full circle, back to the insights and counsel of a wise man, Vilhelm Grønbech. His insights on 'luck as rede' are essential: *luck flows from good counsel, and fails when rede is lacking.* But how are we to judge what counsel is good? Humans (including our own rede to ourselves) and lesser spirits are capable of giving us bad counsel, as well as good. We need criteria to judge what rede is good, and how to act upon it.

This is where ethics and active, experienced interactions and friendship with our Holy Ones comes in, along with other important insights into history, human behavior, and Heathen philosophy and metaphysics. We do this by learning widely, by developing wisdom, by growing in Heathen ethics, troth and frith, by learning from the consequences of our own and others' experiences. *Let us, as wise and honorable Heathens, pursue and focus on understanding luck as 'wise rede, wisdom and good counsel,'* rather than assuming that "luck is supposed to give me everything I want, and if I'm unlucky that means the universe hates me!"

## Conclusion

My take on the question of whether the forcible conversion of Heathens was wyrded or not? I think it was wyrded, but not for the reason that Christians would like to claim. Wyrd is the action of the past upon the present, and is influenced by Skuld or *scyld* / shild: by the debts incurred during those past actions. The past reliance of Heathens on luck being its own justification, on 'might makes right' meant that all of the underhanded, brutal power and might that 'conqueror' Christians brought to bear on them were 'proven to be right, wyrded to happen.' Their over-reliance on luck and power, and under-reliance on Heathen thew, ethics, troth and wisdom led through the paths of wyrd to the outcome of conversion. (Please note that I am greatly oversimplifying the whole situation on both sides, Heathen and Christian! I am trying to draw out and simplify some philosophical principles, rather than provide a detailed history.)

The forcible conversion was an ordeal, guided by the inexorable hands of the Norns. It was the contest type of ordeal, with winners and losers, and the outcome was indeed shaped by wyrd, by past events. This was the action of impersonal wyrd, the flow of events causing other events.

But this was also a deliberate challenge type of ordeal, such as the one Odin put himself through on the Tree. This was and is the challenge given by the Norns, Odin, Tyr, and our other Deities to their followers. *The challenge is to learn wisdom: not just by suffering through and reacting to events, but by learning from them and shaping what-is-to-come accordingly.* That is our task today, as modern Heathens re-establishing the ancient troth.

*Wisdom is shaped into rede,*

*Rede is shaped into luck and deeds,*

*Luck and deeds flow into Wyrd,*

*Wyrd flows back into the world to shape events...*

*...which we come to understand through Wisdom,*
*thus completing the cycle.*

So it is: then, now, and always.

Wyrd flows back into the Worlds to shape events....

Watercolor painting by Dale Wood.

# 7. Weaving It All Together

In this book, I've presented a sequential pattern of ethical development. In the two *Oaths* essays, I discussed a traditional Heathen way to grow our personal power, our might and main, that will help us succeed in the next steps of our ethical growth and development.

In *Threads of Wyrd and Shild,* I offered a ritual framework within which to heal the wounds caused to ourselves and to others by our mistakes, wrongdoing, and unmet moral obligations. Such wounds weaken our own might and main, as well as the might and main of others who have been affected by our deeds or lack of deeds.

In *Heathen Frith* I talked about ways to interweave many people's might and main together, to weave the fabric of frith, of a well-functioning group or community focused on mutual well-being. Such an enterprise is always faced with ongoing challenges. I highlighted some of these challenges so that, through our awareness and understanding of them, we can strive to avoid and work around the pitfalls that are part of the nature of group or community life.

In the introduction to this book, I wrote about the need for wisdom as we seek to live a well-balanced, ethical life. Heathens in the past had a great respect for wisdom, and a rather unique understanding of what it is. One of the main components of wisdom, in their view, was an understanding of wyrd. *Webs of Luck and Wyrd* is an attempt I've made at

133

pursuing such a path of Heathen wisdom, by trying to understand some underlying connections between luck, wyrd, ethics, and events important to Heathen history.

## Distillation

Here, we want to distill our discussion from complexity into simplicity, from philosophical discussions into a few clear points to consider and remember. Recall that 'ethics' refers to 'the tested and time-honored customs of our culture, our values, our ideals, our aspirations.' So what can we draw from these essays, that we can apply as we grow in Heathen might and main, and live our lives the best way we can, here and now? How shall we distill the ethical values I've discussed here?

### *Commitment and the fulfillment of commitments*

I discuss this ethical value in the essays on oathing. What this boils down to is 'will, will-power.' Oathing, commitment, and the actions that fulfill them are movements of the deep Will of our being: the Will that reaches beyond petty surface distractions into the depths of who we truly are. We undertake oaths and commitments both to strengthen our Will, and to express that Will into our Midgard life.

Through these actions, and the might and main that grow from them, we can shape our life to express our greatest values, benefiting ourself and those around us. This can be done even under the most challenging of circumstances. Indeed, as heroes of all times and places and circumstances have found, the greater the challenges, the more potential

134

there is for growing a mighty Will to meet those challenges and rise above them.

### *Clear sight and resolve*

In the discussion of shild, I encouraged the pursuit of clear sight, of truly understanding our mistakes, the wrongs we've done and those done to us, our failings, and the effects these have on our wyrd and ørlög. These matters impact not only ourselves, but many others whose lives are entwined with ours. With that clear sight and understanding, we resolve to address these issues in a responsible way, and by doing so, we resolve them in the best way we can. In the process, we help to untangle our wyrd and lay out new strands of ørlög to influence our future. We become more aware of these deep matters of wyrd, ørlög, shild, and how to work with them to shape an ethical Heathen life.

### *Community*

Humans cannot live and thrive in isolation. Families, groups, community, culture, society, whatever form they might take, are essential for our wellbeing. However necessary they are, though, they come with a lot of baggage, and potential for harm as well as for benefits. Forming and maintaining a strong, healthy community of any size is an ongoing challenge, and requires commitment, clear sight, wisdom, generosity, patience, and many other virtues. It requires an ethos, "the characteristic spirit of a culture, era, or community as manifested in its beliefs and aspirations," as I quoted in the introduction to this book. I believe that the old word 'frith' captures the spirit of that ethos for Heathens. The better we come to understand this complex concept, and practice it in accordance with our values today, the more solid and nurturing our groups and communities become.

## Wisdom and good rede

'Wisdom' is something we weave, strand by strand, from the experiences of our life and our deep thoughts and feelings about those experiences. We weave it from knowledge and experience shared with others, from observation and from learning. Being Heathen, pursuing Heathen philosophy and ethics, adds another dimension of depth to our wisdom.

As we sincerely pursue and practice wisdom in our life, we gradually become able to offer good rede to others, and to ourself as well. We develop our Will, our clear sight, the many qualities needed to establish and maintain frith in our communities. We gain insights into hidden matters of wyrd, ørlög, luck, hamingja, and other spiritual mysteries that shape our lives.

We become known, ourselves, for these virtues we are developing. We gain a good reputation. People trust us: trust our word, our honor, our motivations, our intentions, our wisdom. They come to us for rede and insights, and we share what we have with them. Our efforts help to shape the flow of luck and success in life, especially the luck and success that leads to, and grows from, an ethical Heathen life. *Our ideas of what luck and success really are, are themselves shaped by wisdom and good rede, and we learn to redefine them in ethical, Heathen ways.*

The ethical values I've discussed here are not the only ones that are important for Heathen life, and human life in general. These are a selection, a subset, of ethical values, but I believe they are foundational. I wrote at the beginning that two of the most important Heathen values are the growth of our ethical might and main, and the maintenance of healthy, functional communities. These were greatly valued by Heathens of the past, and I believe are of equally great value for us today. The virtues and qualities that support these aims of ethical personal power and thriving communities, Heathen and non-Heathen, are clearly ones we as Heathens should pursue. These include virtues that have been much discussed in modern Heathenry, such as honor and generosity.

## In closing

Ethics is not, truly, just a set of rules that we follow. Heathen ethics is a way of being, a world-view. In the past, this world-view and way of being was, to an extent, interrupted by historical events. Even if it had not been interrupted, it would have evolved and changed over the centuries between then and now, but perhaps the underlying philosophy would have been better maintained and evolved to fit the changing times.

That is not how things happened, and so it falls to us as modern Heathens to look deeply into what was valuable in the Heathen past, and ask whether there is still value there, that can be adapted to enrich and empower present-day Heathen life. This is the project that I am dedicated to, and pursue in many different areas: Heathen soul lore, Heathen ethics, Heathen life-ways, Heathen philosophy and metaphysics. This book will be followed by a book about ørlög, which will have a good deal of relevance to the subjects discussed in this book, as well.

I hope that what I have written here is thought-provoking for you, no matter what direction your thoughts take you! Whether you agree with my conclusions or not, the topics I have written about here are worth the time and effort for all of us to consider. Each of us must explore our own paths of wisdom and experience, but it is worthwhile to share what we learn along the way, and work together to grow modern Heathen world-views and practices that support us all in frith and fruitfulness.

# Afterword: Ethics, Ideals, and Vilhelm Grønbech

I drew a number of points in these essays from Vilhelm Grønbech's volumes on *The Culture of the Teutons.* Modern academics sometimes criticize Grønbech's study of Heathen culture for being overly idealized, and taking evidence farther than is academically justified. This may be true. I treasure Grønbech for his ability to inspire, for the very idealization that academics may criticize.

The field of ethics *needs* idealization: *ethics are ideals that we strive to achieve as individuals and as a society.* To me, that's the difference between 'laws' and 'ethics,' though obviously they are related.

Laws say "this is how you have to do things."

Ethics say "here is how you strive to be a person of goodness and honor, to earn the respect of others and your own self-respect, by following a code of conduct that you evaluate yourself and accept as good and right."

Laws are codified records, while ethics are ideals implanted and nurtured within our souls. I think Grønbech had deep roots in the Heathen spirit, whatever his outer religious beliefs. I consider him more as a modern Heathen-minded philosopher than as a precise historian. His insights offer many riches for modern Heathens to consider as we define new folkways for a modern Heathenism, even if his historical conclusions are sometimes overblown.

139

Drawing by Dale Wood.

# Word-Hoard / Glossary

**Alf (sing.), Alfar (pl.):** This term can refer to a divine tribe of beings closely associated with the Æsir Gods, and is also used to designate the spirits of deceased male ancestors.

**Dis (sing.), Disir (pl.):** Literal meaning is a lady or a noblewoman; sometimes a demi-goddess. Most commonly used to indicate the spirits of one's deceased female ancestors.

**Fylgja:** The *fylgja* (meaning 'follower') is a spirit who is closely associated with a living person throughout their life. It may take an animal form, and serve as a guardian.

**Hamingja:** In Norse folklore, Hamingja is both a form of luck, and a spirit who bears and gives that luck to the person with whom it is associated. The Hamingja is considered to reside in the womb / caul / afterbirth. It accompanies the child it was born with throughout life, as long as nothing dire occurs to destroy its luck or its connection to the person.

**Hvergelmir:** In Norse mythology, a well or wellspring located in the cold, Niflheim side of Ginnungagap, under a root of the World-Tree, from which the Elivagar river(s) flows. In my thought, Hvergelmir is centered in Ginnungagap and is the source of the energy flows that form the cosmos.

**Mægen, megin, main:** Power, force, energy that is inherent in living beings, magical objects, and otherworldly beings. Used in a modern Heathen context, it often implies spiritual power gained from living an ethical Heathen life.

**Midgard:** The World of Earth and all it encompasses. It means 'middle yard, enclosure', a word and meaning that existed in all the Germanic languages, often in the form of 'middle earth' meanings. This term implies an assumption that there are 'upper' and 'lower' worlds as well. According to Norse lore, Midgard was formed from the Giant Ymir's sacrificed body by Odin, Vili and Ve.

**Mimir and his Well:** Mimir is an ancient, wise Giant, the mentor and perhaps the maternal uncle of Odin. He was beheaded while a hostage with the Vanir, but Odin preserved his head and continues to receive wise rede from it. Mimir's Well is considered a place of great wisdom and mystery. Odin pledged his eye to this well in exchange for runic knowledge, and the well also is said to contain Heimdal's horn and his hearing or his ear. My idea is that Mimir's Head / Well is 'World-Mind' or the Noösphere, the realm where Thought occurs.

**Niflheim:** In Norse lore, the cold, icy end of the primal space called Ginnungagap. The word means 'mist-world'. In my thought, the term Niflheim describes the mist of spiritual proto-being, the field of Ahma, that continually arises from Ginnungagap, generated by the primal polarities of Ice and

Fire. This mist is the basis for all subsequent shapings of worlds and beings.

**Norns:** Three womanly beings, possibly Giants though their origins are unclear. In Norse lore they are named Urðr, Verðandi, and Skuld, representing 'What-Is', 'What Is Becoming', and 'Debt, or What Should Be.' They live beside the Well of Wyrd / destiny, called Urðarbrunnr, and nourish the World-Tree with mud and water from the Well. They speak ørlög or fate for humans, and the council or doom-stead of the Gods takes place near their Well; presumably they participate in these councils. There are also lesser norns, who appear as fairy godmothers and similar beings involved with people's fates. In Anglo-Saxon, the Norns are called the Wyrdæ, named Wyrd, Werthende and Scyld (the latter two names are translated from Norse, not attested in Anglo-Saxon writings).

**Ordeal:** An "or-deal" in a Heathen philosophical sense means *the primal roots of a given ordeal-circumstance: the ørlög, the weaving of wyrd, which has been dealt out for one to face here and now, in this place, in this time.'* An 'ordeal' has the connotation of a struggle, a challenge, a personal testing, and it is that, but it is more. It is fateful, it is a weaving of wyrd, a drawing-together of the strands of our life into a nexus-point of deep significance. Much of our past has gone into reaching this nexus-point of the ordeal, and much will lead forth from its outcome, that will shape our time to come. (In other words, an ordeal is a really big deal!)

In my understanding of Heathen philosophy, life itself is an ordeal in this sense: a complex, patterned knot or nexus of strands of ørlög, arising from the past, gathered together in the present, and shaping the future to come. The ordeal of life is a challenge and a struggle, indeed, but more than that, it shapes the whole pattern of our Being, and shapes the meaning that our life holds.

Our purpose in life is not to avoid or escape true Heathen ordeals, but to rise to the challenge they offer: the challenge not only to meet the ordeal successfully, but to use that challenge to emerge from the ordeal with greater soul-qualities than we had when we went into it. This is the 'path of the hero' in Germanic culture.

**Ørlög, Orlay:** This word means the 'ur-layers, primal layers', and is related to the words for 'law.' These layers are laid by the Norns, shaped from the deeds and events of humankind and Midgard, as well as the other Worlds and beings. In turn, ørlög influences the lives and life-spans of living humans. Ørlög is the Old Norse term, orlæg or orlay is Anglo-Saxon.

**Ragnarök:** 'The destiny or fate of the Gods,' a great battle between the Gods and the Jotnar or Giants, with the dead from different realms participating on different sides. Some modern Heathens regard Ragnarök as having already happened, in the form of the forcible conversions from Heathenism to Christianity during the early Middle Ages. Others regard it as an event yet to come, and some see

Ragnarok as a cyclical, recurrent event, having already happened in the past, and still to come again in the future.

**Rede:** 'Rede' refers to advice, counsel, guidance, but also to one's own rede to oneself: one's experience, learning, thought, intuitions applied to solve problems, meet challenges, and generally conduct one's life successfully. Wise rede leads to wise actions, luck, and success. Our ancient kin easily recognized those who were 'rede-y,' guided by wise rede whether from others or within themselves, versus those who were 'unrede-y' and just seemed to get everything wrong no matter how hard they seemed to try. When this unrede-y person was a king, this spelled disaster for his reign.

"The ancient word rede...is a perfect illustration of Teutonic psychology. When given to others, it means counsel; when applied to the luck working within the mind, it means wisdom, or a good plan, and from an ethical point of view, just and honest thoughts. But the word naturally includes the idea of success, which accompanies wise and upright devising, and on the other hand power and authority, which are the working of a sound will." (Grønbech p. 148)

**Spaecraft, spaework:** In modern Heathen terminology, these words refer to a practice of oracular trance work, often performed in a group setting, other times performed individually, to explore questions and issues of interest to the querents. Such trance-working in pursuit of wisdom and insights can also be done on one's own behalf.

**Sumble, sumbel, symbel:** A Heathen ritual of community, where participants sit together and make toasts, boasts and oaths, offer prayers, remembrances, poetry or songs, give gifts, and witness events such as agreements, betrothals or weddings, new members being sworn in or accepted to the group, anniversaries, and the like. Sacred drinks, often imbibed from drinking horns, are raised and drunk from to hail and acknowledge the words spoken in sumble. Among modern Heathens, usually the first round of drinks and speeches hails the Deities, the second hails ancestors and heroes, those we admire and are grateful toward. The third and any subsequent rounds are 'speaker's choice' as to subject matter. Some Heathens consider that the words spoken in sumble are 'laid in the Well of Wyrd.' Therefore, great care should be taken in considering one's words, especially with regard to oaths and commitments, since they are likely to become part of wyrd and have powerful impacts on our lives. (See Chapter 13 in Waggoner for more detail about sumbel or sumble.)

**Syn:** The Goddess Syn wards the doors of the hall, and closes them against those who must not enter. She is called on at the Thingsteads (assemblies) when one wishes to refute an accusation, and is considered the Goddess of Denial. (*Gylfaginning* p. 30, Edda). I call her the "Just Say No" Goddess, the one who helps us protect our healthy and necessary boundaries against intrusion.

**Thew, thews:** Customs and norms of behavior; ethical norms. This is the original meaning of the word; more recently it came to mean physical strength, and the tendons and ligaments that make our limbs and muscles work together powerfully. Both meanings combine well for the practice of Heathen ethics—the exercise of our might and main applied to the challenges of daily life in ethical ways. (See Waggoner, Chapter 3, for more about Heathen ethics.)

**Thyle, Thul or Thulr:** In modern Heathenry this person is, in effect, both master of ceremonies and master of arms at a sumble. He or she must be a person of wise judgement and good reputation, and an experienced and knowledgeable Heathen. Their function at sumble is to monitor oaths and promises by challenging and testing anyone who proposes to swear an oath, as to their ability to follow through with the oath. They must also moderate any arguments or challenges that might occur, and handle any conflicts appropriately, according to the values and customs of the group who is hosting the sumble. People proposing to make an oath in sumble are advised to consult with the Thyle beforehand; this helps the process to go smoothly. It should be noted that not all Heathen groups make use of a Thyle at sumble; some consider it unnecessary. (See Chapter 13 in Waggoner for more detail about the Thyle's role in sumble.)

**Werold:** A word meaning 'man-age', used in Anglo-Saxon, Old Saxon and Old High German, and referring to the totality of a person's life-span and life-experience. In Old Norse, the word is Veraldr.

**Wode:** One of the gifts given by Hœnir / Odin's brother when two trees or logs were transformed into the humans Ask and Embla. Wode refers to an ecstatic state of heightened spiritual—and sometimes physical—energy, which can take forms ranging from inspired eloquence and prophecy, artistic and intellectual genius, warrior focus and strength, to berserker rage, or outright madness. I see the gift of wode as a divine spark or a bridge, that enables humans to reach divine consciousness and communication with the Deities. If the person is not fit nor prepared for this, if their motives are skewed, or if they approach the Deities in inappropriate, offensive ways, the resulting flow of wode may backfire into negative forms.

**World-Tree, Yggdrasil:** The cosmic Tree, the structure of Space and all that exists within space. It is rooted in the three great Wells of power in Norse myth: Hvergelmir, Mimir's Well, and Urðr's Well, and the Nine Worlds are supported by its branches and roots.

**Worlds, Nine Worlds:** Norse mythology envisions nine worlds as the home-bases for different kinds of beings: Asgard for the Æsir, Vanaheim for the Vanir, Alfheim for the Alfar or elves, Midgard for humans, Svartalfheim for the Dwarves, Hel for the dead, Jotunheim for the Giants, and the Worlds of the primal energies: the World of ice and cold, Niflheim, and the World of Fire, Muspelheim.

**Wyrd, and Well of:** Wyrd is an Anglo-Saxon word derived from 'to become, to happen, to come to pass'; basically, 'to come into being.' This is the name of a being or a power that brings about destiny and fate in Anglo-Saxon lore, in particular, the circumstances of one's death. Wyrd is cognate with Norse Norn-name Urðr, and Wyrd's Well is the same as Urðarbrunnr: the Well of Fate (approximately). 'Fate, Destiny' and 'Wyrd' are not exactly the same, but overlap a good deal in meaning. This is an oversimplification; there is much more to be learned about wyrd!

**Yggdrasil:** The 'steed of Ygg'. 'Ygg' means the 'terrible one', and is a byname of Odin. His 'steed' here is the World-Tree upon which he hung for nine days and nights to win the Runes.

# Book-Hoard / Bibliography

Bauschatz, Paul. *The Well and the Tree: World and Time in Early Germanic Culture.* The University of Massachusetts Press, Amherst, 1982.

Davidson, Hilda Ellis. *The Lost Beliefs of Modern Europe.* Routledge, New York, 1993.

DeVries, Jan. *Altgermansche Religionsgeschichte* vol. I. Walter de Gruyter & Co., Berlin, 1956.

*Eyrbyggja Saga.* Hermann Palsson and Paul Edwards, translators, Penguin Books, London, England, 1989.

Garmonsway, G. N., transl. *The Anglo-Saxon Chronicle.* Everyman's Library, London, England, 1972.

Griffiths, Bill. *An Introduction to Early English Law.* Anglo-Saxon Books, Norfolk, England, 1995.

Griffiths, Bill. *The Battle of Maldon.* Anglo-Saxon Books, Middlesex, England, 1991.

Grimm, Jacob. *Teutonic Mythology.* J.S. Stalleybrass edition. George Bell & Sons, London, 1883.

150

Grønbech, Vilhelm. *The Culture of the Teutons.* Humphrey Milford, Oxford University Press, London, 1931.

Hall, J.R. Clark. *A Concise Anglo-Saxon Dictionary, 4th Edition.* University of Toronto Press, Toronto, 1960.

Linsell, Tony. *Anglo-Saxon Mythology, Migration and Magic.* Anglo-Saxon Books, Middlesex, England, 1994.

*Our Troth, 2nd Edition, Vol. 1: History and Lore.* Compiled by Kveldulf Hagan Gundarsson and others. The Troth, Oldsmar FL, 2006.

Russell, James C. *The Germanization of Early Medieval Christianity: A Sociohistorical Approach to Religious Transformation.* Oxford University Press, New York, 1994.

Rose, Winifred Hodge. "Images of Orlay," and "A Short Blog on Ørlög and Wyrd," at https://heathensoullore.net/

Sturlason, Snorri. "History of Olaf Tryggvason" in *Heimskringla or the Lives of the Norse Kings* , edited with notes by Erling Monsen and translated with the assistance of A.H. Smith, Dover Publications, Inc, New York, 1990.

Waggoner, Ben, and others. *Our Troth 3rd Edition, Vol. 3: Heathen Life.* The Troth, Philadelphia PA, 2022.

Our Mimir-shrine, a stone head carved by my husband.
It sits above a small pond on our land, overshadowed by a
great, spreading Yew.  Mimir and his Well represent
wisdom, memory, and inspiration.

# About the Author

Winifred Hodge Rose is an Elder of the Troth, an inclusive, international Heathen organization. She has followed a Heathen path for more than thirty years, serving as a scholar, writer, leader, teacher, priestess, and oracular spaewife in many Heathen venues.

   Winifred grew up as the daughter of a US diplomat stationed in various countries during the 1950s and 1960s, and later lived for years in Greece and Germany. These experiences enabled her to learn foreign languages through immersion, and to develop the ability to observe and adapt to different cultures and world-views. This has stood her in good stead in her efforts to understand, as well as possible, ancient Heathen world-views and adapt them for modern Heathen use.

Winifred is retired from her career as a research scientist working on methods for watershed and natural resources management on military installations in the US and Germany. She has two grown children and three growing grandsons, and lives with her blacksmith husband in the Illinois countryside.

Winifred published her first Heathen book, *Heathen Soul Lore Foundations: Ancient and Modern Germanic Pagan Concepts of the Souls*, in 2021. Her second book, *Heathen Soul Lore: A Personal Approach,* was published in 2022, along with a children's illustrated story and activity book, *Idunn's Trees: A New Tale of the Norse Goddess Idunn.* Her website, with many articles, poems and songs, ceremonies, meditations, fiction and more, can be found at *HeathenSoulLore.net.*

# A Word about Wordfruma Press

*Fruma* means 'origin, beginning' in Anglo-Saxon, and *ordfruma* means the fount or the source. The Anglo-Saxon word *Os* refers to a God of the Esa or Æsir tribe, and the Rune Poem for the rune Os goes as follows:

> *Os is 'ordfruma' of every speech,*
> *The support of wisdom and the benefit of the wise,*
> *And for every earl, prosperity and hope.*
> (my translation)

The *Os,* the Esa-God referred to, is Woden or Odin, the fount and origin of speech, eloquence and wisdom. Since my work relies in large part on understanding the roots and sources of words, I have made a play on words here, changing *ordfruma* to *wordfruma:* "the origin of words". The origin or wellspring of meaningful words flows from godly inspiration: a divine gift that underlies the formation and emergence of our entire species, *homo sapiens.* Wordfruma Press thus honors the gift of speech, and the origins of the gift: all of the Holy Ones.

The trademark logo pictured here, conceptualized by myself and created by Forest Hawkins, shows the rune Ansuz, the Proto-Germanic name of the rune Os, rising up from a wellspring. Ansuz takes shape as a fountain that represents the power of speech and wisdom. The shape of the logo also represents the Well of Wyrd and the World-Tree, with dew from the Tree dropping into the Well.

Wordfruma Press publishes scholarly and inspirational Heathen works.

# Other Publications from Wordfruma Press

*Heathen Soul Lore Foundations: Ancient and Modern Germanic Pagan Concepts of the Souls,* 2021 (575 pages)

*Heathen Soul Lore: A Personal Approach,* 2022 (423 pages)

*Idunn's Trees: A New Tale of the Norse Goddess Idunn,* 2022 (children's illustrated story and activity book, 52 pages)

*Mothers-Night Blot and Yule Celebration, with Heathen Words for Yule Songs,* 2022 (booklet, 28 pages)

TM

WordfrumaPress.com

HeathenSoulLore.net

www.ingramcontent.com/pod-product-compliance
Lightning Source LLC
Chambersburg PA
CBHW071443090426
42737CB00011B/1763